KNIT 'N' FELT BAGS

KNIT 'N' FELT BAGS

20 QUICK-AND-EASY EMBELLISHED BAGS

BEV BEATTIE

TRAFALGAR SQUARE
North Pomfret, Vermont

First published in the United States of America in 2009 by Trafalgar Square Books North Pomfret, Vermont 05053

Printed and bound in China

This book was conceived and produced by Breslich & Foss Ltd, London

Photography: **Sussie Bell**
Design: **Elizabeth Healey**
Commissioning editor:
  Janet Ravenscroft
Project manager: **Kate Haxell**

ISBN 978-1-57076-440-0

Library of Congress Catalog Card Number 2009003526

10 9 8 7 6 5 4 3 2 1

contents

introduction

I discovered felting when a friend gave me some very thick pure wool, almost like a roving. I had to knit this wool on very thick needles, like broom handles, and this very large bag started to appear. Then came the exciting bit: I put it in the washing machine. I found myself standing waiting for the washing machine to finish—how crazy is that!

When I opened the washing machine door, this very large bag that I thought would hold my big college portfolio had become a shallow knitting-needle bag. Not being a person to let this go, I made another one, and another one, until I had a bag of the correct proportions. I loved it, but by then the wool had run out.

I bought various pure wool yarns, or so-called pure wools. I found that many of these wools had been treated chemically or were super-wash wool, and so they would not felt. That is where the wonders of the Internet came into play. I sourced wool yarns from all over the world, found the perfect yarn for what I wanted and started to make more and more bags. There was no going back now.

I took a few bags into college to show my classmates and one of the students, Jenny, wanted to buy a bag. I was absolutely stunned when she offered me the money there and then. A few days later another lady, Tanya, wanted to buy a different bag, and I realized that maybe these bags could sell.

The secret is in the wool yarn: if you have good wool, the bags work.

My mom, Doreen, and my sisters, Bridget and Bernadette, took my bags to their friends, work, hairdressers, and many other places. They were great sales staff and I was selling bags as fast as I could knit them. I was buying pounds of yarn and friends at college asked to buy that, too, and that is where my yarn business, Knitting4fun, started.

Soon after that I attended a knitting and stitching show and, realizing that I could not knit enough bags to keep up with the demand, I made up a few kits with the wool yarns, needles, and pattern needed to make the bags. These all sold and each evening after the show I had to make up more and more kits. My husband, Tom, and his friend, David, built my website and the business grew. This is why we now have yarn in every room of the house, except the bathroom (you could get a lot of yarn in that bath though!).

The great thing about knitting and felting is that it's quick and easy to do and is very forgiving. Once the knitting is felted you cannot see that your gauge isn't perfect, that you may have dropped a stitch, or any other small mistakes in the knitting. Beginners and the more experienced alike will get excellent results.

The secret is in the wool yarn: if you have good wool, the bags work. The wools I use felt at 40 degrees in the washing machine. This low-temperature felting is why I can incorporate the acrylic and fancy yarns without fear of anything being ruined in the wash.

I hope you enjoy knitting and felting your own bags as much as I do.

Bev Beattie

Once the knitting is felted you cannot see that your gauge isn't perfect, that you may have dropped a stitch, or any other small mistakes in the knitting.

bucket bags

This style of bag is very simple and quick to knit—perfect for novice knitters to try. The bucket shape works well with longer handles that you can sling over your shoulder, so the bags are practical carry-alls as well as stylish accessories.

pure purple

You will need

- 4½oz of Knitting4fun Pure Wool in Purple (A)
- 1¾oz of Elle Pizzazz in Poison 252 (B)
- 4½oz of Knitting4fun Pure Wool in Damson (C)
- US 11 (24 in. long) circular needle
- US 15 (24 in. or 32 in. long) circular needle
- Set of five US 15 double-pointed needles
- Knitter's sewing needle or bodkin for sewing
- Large snap (optional)

Finished size

Bag measures approx 9½ in. high by 9 in. wide.

This was one of the first bags I ever made. I love the Elle Pizzazz yarn and wanted to use it to make a dramatically textured bag.

The shape of this bag was originally inspired by a hat pattern: imagine it upside down and smaller! The revised pattern is so easy to knit and can be adapted to make a bag of any size, small or large.

This bag was made with two different shades of purple yarn knitted together to give a slightly variegated effect. This complements the mix of colors in the textured yarn making the wonderful fringe around the top of the bag.

The decreases for the bottom of the bag are made on double-pointed needles. Knitted i-cord handles complete the bag, and these can be knitted almost any length to suit your needs.

Gauge

12 stitches and 14 rows to
4 in. over st st on US 15
needles using two strands of
A held together, although
gauge is not crucial in felting.

Abbreviations

See page 125.

Bag

Using US 11 circular needle and one strand each of A and B held together, cast on 65 sts.

Join the cast on row into a circle, ensuring that the knitting is not twisted, and place a marker to establish the beginning of the round.

Purl 8 to 10 rounds, or until the trim at the top of the bag is the desired depth. Purling the stitches helps to keep the textured yarn on the right side of the knitting. Tease out the long fibers as you work so that they do not get trapped in the knitted fabric.

Break off B and join in a strand of C.

Change to US 15 circular needle and cont in knit stitch.

Next round: [K12, inc] five times. (70 sts)

Knit 45 rounds using one strand each of A and C held together.

Shape base

Slip marker to the right-hand needle and start the shaping as folls:

Next round: [K8, k2tog] to the end of the round. (63 sts)

Knit 3 rounds.

Next round: [K7, k2tog] to the end of the round. (56 sts)

Knit 2 rounds.

Change to US 15 double-pointed needles as folls:

Next round: *[K6, k2tog] twice onto one double-pointed needle; rep from * onto two more needles then k6, k2tog once onto the fourth needle. (49 sts)

Cont shaping on double-pointed needles as folls:

Knit 1 round.

Next round: [K5, k2tog] to the end of the round. (42 sts)

Next round: [K4, k2tog] to the end of the round. (35 sts)

Next round: [K3, k2tog] to the end of the round. (28 sts)

Next round: [K2, k2tog] to the end of the round. (21 sts)

Next round: [K1, k2tog] to the end of the round. (14 sts)

Next round: [K2tog] to the end of the round. (7 sts)

Leaving a 15 in. tail, cut yarn. Thread tail through rem sts. Thread tail into knitter's sewing needle and sew through these sts several times to secure the end.

Handles (make two)

Using US 15 double-pointed needles and two strands of A held together (or one strand each of A and C held together if you prefer), cast on 4 sts.

Knit 1 row.

Switch needles in your hands, so the needle with the stitches on is in your left hand again. Slide the stitches to the other end of the needle and, pulling the yarn across the back of the stitches, knit the row again. The first three or four rows will be flat but don't worry, after that the knitting will become tubular. Before knitting the first stitch of each row, give the yarn a tug to make the strand across the back disappear.

Cont in this way, sliding and knitting, until the handle is the required length. As the handles will shrink by approximately one-third during felting, I usually knit about 50–60 rows for a short hand-held handle, 100 rows for a longer hand-held handle, and 120–140 rows for a shoulder handle.

Bind off.

To finish

Using the knitter's sewing needle and A, sew the handles to the inside of the trim section at the top of the bag, about ½ in. down from the top edge.

Darn in all loose ends.

Following the instructions on pages 123–124, machine-wash the bag to felt it.

You can sew on a large snap to fasten the bag if desired.

This bag was made with two different shades of purple yarn knitted together to give a slightly variegated effect. This complements the mix of colors in the textured yarn making the wonderful fringe around the top of the bag.

plant pot

You will need

- 5¼oz of Knitting4fun Pure Wool in Rust (A)
- 3½oz of Colinette Giotto in Windfall 149 (B)
- Small amounts of Knitting4fun Pure Wool in Apple Green, Yellow, and Cream
- US 11 (16 in. or 24 in. long) circular needle
- US 13 (24 in. long) circular needle
- Set of four US 13 double-pointed needles
- Pair of US 10 knitting needles
- J/10 crochet hook
- Knitter's sewing needle or bodkin for sewing
- Large snap (optional)

Finished size

Bag measures approx 7 in. high by 7 in. wide.

The lovingly tended potted plants in my mother's garden inspired me to design this bag. The mixture of the rust-colored pure wool yarn and the variegated ribbon yarn gives the look of the weathering on her terracotta pots.

Small sprays of knitted leaves tumble down the sides of the bag, with crocheted buds and flowers growing from them. Add a couple of leaves and flowers to the handles, too, for a finishing touch. This pattern can be made with flowers in any colors to make a very pretty and dainty bag.

The bag can be made without a handle and used as a plant pot holder. It would be lovely with flowers crocheted in colors to match the potted plant placed in it, or to coordinate with your room décor.

Gauge

14 stitches and 16 rows to 4 in. over st st on US 13 needles using one strand each of A and B held together, although gauge is not crucial in felting.

Abbreviations

See page 125.

Bag

Using US 11 circular needle and one strand each of A and B held together, cast on 55 sts.

Join the cast on row into a circle, ensuring that the knitting is not twisted, and place a marker to establish the beginning of the round.

Round 1: [K1, p1] to last st, k1.

Round 2: [P1, k1] to last st, p1.

Rep rounds 1–2 once more then rep round 1 once more.

Round 6: [K10, inc] five times. (60 sts)

Change to US 13 circular needle and cont in knit stitch.

Knit 35 rounds.

Shape base

Slip marker to the right-hand needle and start the shaping as folls:

Round 42: [K8, k2tog] to the end of the round. (54 sts)

Knit 2 rounds.

Round 45: [K7, k2tog] to the end of the round. (48 sts)

Knit 2 rounds.

Change to US 13 double-pointed needles as folls:

Round 48: *[K6, k2tog] twice onto one double-pointed needle; rep from * onto two more needles. (42 sts)

Cont shaping on double-pointed needles as folls:

Knit 1 round.

Round 50: [K5, k2tog] to the end of the round. (36 sts)

Round 51: [K4, k2tog] to the end of the round. (30 sts)

Round 52: [K3, k2tog] to the end of the round. (24 sts)

Round 53: [K2, k2tog] to the end of the round. (18 sts)

Round 54: [K1, k2tog] to the end of the round. (12 sts)

Round 55: [K2tog] to the end of the round. (6 sts)

Leaving a 15 in. tail, cut yarn. Thread tail through rem sts. Thread tail into knitter's sewing needle and sew through these sts several times to secure the end.

Handle (make one)

Using US 13 double-pointed needles and one strand of A, cast on 4 sts.
Knit 1 row.

Switch needles in your hands, so the needle with the stitches on is in your left hand again. Slide the stitches to the other end of the needle and, pulling the yarn across the back of the stitches, knit the row again. The first three or four rows will be flat but don't worry, after that the knitting will become tubular. Before knitting the first stitch of each row, give the yarn a tug to make the strand across the back disappear.

Cont in this way, sliding and knitting, until the handle is the required length. As the handles will shrink by approximately one-third during felting, I usually knit about 50–60 rows for a short hand-held handle, 100 rows for a longer hand-held handle, and 120–140 rows for a shoulder handle.

Bind off.

Trailing leaves

Using US 10 knitting needles and one strand of Apple Green Pure Wool, cast on 7 sts.

Row 1: *Bind off 6 sts, slip rem st onto the left-hand needle and cast on 6 sts; rep from * to make a long chain of leaves. Vary the length of the leaves by casting on more or fewer sts, always binding off until 1 st is left.

When chain is desired length, fasten off.

Crochet flower

Using J/10 crochet hook and one strand of Yellow Pure Wool, chain 5, join with a slip st to form a ring.

Change to Cream Pure Wool and make 10 sc in ring.

Join.

Chain 3, make 3 dc in next st, chain 2, sc in next st.

Repeat from * to * around ring four more times to make five petals.

Fasten off, leaving a 20 in. tail.

To finish

Drape the chain of trailing leaves around the bag and sew it in place using the knitter's sewing needle and matching yarn.

Using matching yarn, sew the flowers in place.

Using A, sew the handle to the inside of the top of the bag, about ½ in. down from the top edge.

Darn in all loose ends.

Following the instructions on pages 123–124, machine-wash the bag to felt it.

You can sew on a large snap to fasten the bag if desired.

flower power

You will need

- 5¼oz of Knitting4fun
  Pure Wool in
  Lime Green (A)
- 3½oz of Colinette Giotto
  in Lagoon 138 (B)
- Small amount of
  Knitting4fun Pure Wool in
  Turquoise (C)
- Beads for embellishing
  flowers
- US 11 (16 in. or 24 in. long)
  circular needle
- US 13 (24 in. long)
  circular needle
- Set of four US 13
  double-pointed needles
- G/6 crochet hook
- Pair of US 10
  knitting needles
- Knitter's sewing needle or
  bodkin for sewing
- Large snap (optional)

Finished size

Bag measures approx 8½ in.
high by 8½ in. wide.

While on vacation a few years ago, I found in a local store a small lavender bag made from silk. It was meant to be hung in the wardrobe, but I thought it was too beautiful to be hidden away. It was that bag that inspired this one.

I decided to make this bag in two of my favorite colors—lime-green and turquoise. The clean, fresh colors evoke the summer and sunshine for me, and remind me of my trips abroad.

I love the way that the wool yarn felts with the ribbon yarns, giving a sheen to the surface of the bag. Crystal beads sewn into the centers of the small turquoise flowers add a little sparkle.

Make this pattern as a bag, or as a holder filled with your favorite pot pourri to hang in your room.

paint box bag

You will need

- 14oz in total of Knitting4fun
  Pure Wool consisting of
  small amounts of Black (A),
  Sunshine Yellow (B),
  Purple (C), Orange (D),
  Bright Green (E), Red (F),
  Royal Blue (G), Turquoise (H),
  Dark Green (I), Fuchsia
  Pink (J), and Lime Green (K)
- US 11 (24 in. long)
  circular needle
- US 15 (32 in. long)
  circular needle
- Set of five US 15
  double-pointed needles
- Knitter's sewing needle or
  bodkin for sewing
- Large snap (optional)

Finished size

Bag measures approx 11 in.
high by 12 in. wide.

On a cold, dreary weekend in winter I bought a paint box and crayon set to keep the children busy. The set included a mosaic-style coloring book that the children filled in with cheerful, bright colors, and it was that which got me thinking about this bag.

I did not plan the colors, I just knitted them as they came to me: it was quite a freeform project. I made the bobbles as I was knitting the bag, but also added more texture by embroidering French knots afterwards, as I decided I wanted more contrast colors in some areas.

I had initially thought of adding brightly colored buttons on some of the stripes, but after I had made the bobbles and added the embroidery, I decided that I would leave the buttons for another bag.

Gauge

12 stitches and 14 rows to 4 in. over st st on US 15 needles using two strands of A held together, although gauge is not crucial in felting.

Abbreviations

MB = make bobble: in contrast color (k1, p1, k1) into next st, turn p3, turn k3, turn p3, turn sk2po, slip the stitch back onto the left-hand needle and knit into it again using main color; cut contrast yarn, pull ends of contrast yarn tight to form the bobble, knot ends together, and sew them into the back of the bobble before felting.
See also page 125.

Note: use two strands of yarn held together throughout unless otherwise stated. Cut yarns between stripes and sew ends in before felting.

Bag

Using US 11 circular needle and two strands of A, cast on 75 sts.

Join the cast on row into a circle, ensuring that the knitting is not twisted, and place a marker to establish the beginning of the round.

Round 1: [K1, p1] to last st, k1.

Round 2: [P1, k1] to last st, p1.

Rep rounds 1–2 twice more.

Round 7: [K14, inc] five times. (80 sts)

Change to US 13 circular needle and cont in knit stitch.

Knit 2 rounds in B.

Round 10 (bobble round): [K7 in B, MB in C] to the end of the round.

Knit 2 rounds in B.

Knit 3 rounds in D.

Round 16: [K4 in E, sl 1 st in D] to the end of the round.

Rep round 16 once more.

Knit 2 rounds in E.

Knit 2 rounds in F.

Round 22: In F [k7, M1] to the end of the round. (90 sts)

Knit 3 rounds in G.

Round 26 (bobble round): [K4 in G, MB in H] to the end of the round.

Knit 3 rounds in G.

Knit 3 rounds in B.

Round 33: [K4 in I, sl 1 st in B] to the end of the round.

Rep round 33 once more.

Knit 3 rounds in J.

Knit 2 rounds in K.

Round 40: In C [k9, M1] to the end of the round. (100 sts)

Knit 2 rounds in C.

Round 43 (bobble round): *K4 in C, MB in F, k4 in C, MB with one strand of D; rep from * to the end of the round.

Knit 2 rounds in C.

Knit 3 rounds in H.

Knit 3 rounds in B.

Round 52: [K4 in J, sl 1 st in B] to the end of the round.

Knit 3 rounds in I.

Knit 2 rounds in E.

Round 58 (bobble round): [K9 in E, MB in L] to the end of the round.

Knit 1 round in E.

Shape base

Slip marker to the right-hand needle and start the shaping as folls:

Round 60: In E [k8, k2tog] to the end of the round. (90 sts)

Knit 3 rounds in K.

Round 64: [K2 in C, sl 1 st in K] to the end of the round.

Rep round 64 twice more.

Knit 1 round in J.

Round 68: In J [k7, k2tog] to the end of the round. (80 sts)

Knit 1 round in G.

Change to US 15 double-pointed needles as folls:

Round 48: *[K6, k2tog] three times onto one double-pointed needle; rep from * onto one more needle, **[K6, k2tog] twice onto next double-pointed needle; rep from ** onto last needle. (70 sts)

Cont shaping on double-pointed needles as folls:

Knit 1 round in G.

Round 50: In F [k5, k2tog] to the end of the round. (60 sts)

Knit 1 round in F.

Round 51: In B [k4, k2tog] to the end of the round. (50 sts)

Knit 1 round in B.

Round 52: In G [k3, k2tog] to the end of the round. (40 sts)

Round 53: In G [k2, k2tog] to the end of the round. (30 sts)

Round 54: In K [k1, k2tog] to the end of the round. (20 sts)

Round 55: In K [k2tog] to the end of the round. (10 sts)

Leaving a 15 in. tail, cut yarn. Thread tail through rem sts. Thread tail into knitter's sewing needle and sew through these sts several times to secure the end.

I did not plan the colors, I just knitted them as they came to me: it was quite a freeform project.

Handles (make two)

Using US 15 double-pointed needles and two strands of A held together, cast on 5 sts.

Knit 1 row.

Switch needles in your hands, so the needle with the stitches on is in your left hand again. Slide the stitches to the other end of the needle and, pulling the yarn across the back of the stitches, knit the row again. The first three or four rows will be flat but don't worry, after that the knitting will become tubular. Before knitting the first stitch of each row, give the yarn a tug to make the strand across the back disappear.

Cont in this way, sliding and knitting, until the handle is the required length. As the handles will shrink by approximately one-third during felting, I usually knit about 50–60 rows for a short hand-held handle, 100 rows for a longer hand-held handle, and 120–140 rows for a shoulder handle.

Bind off.

To finish

Using the knitter's sewing needle and yarns of your choice, add embroidery stitches such as French knots (the small dots on this bag) to the knitting.

Using the knitter's sewing needle and A, sew the handles to the inside of the top of the bag, about ½ in. down from the top edge.

Darn in all loose ends.

Following the instructions on pages 123–124, machine-wash the bag to felt it.

You can sew on a large snap to fasten the bag if desired.

flat-bottomed bags

These bags use a three-needle bind-off to close
the base seam and so complete them. Once felted,
this bind off is almost invisible, making your bag
appear seamless.

jazzy bag

You will need

- 8¾oz of Knitting4fun Pure merino Wool in Turquoise (A)
- 1¾oz of Elle Pizzazz in Carnival 253 (B)
- 1¾oz of Ice Long Eyelash in Fuchsia (C)
- US 11 (16 in. or 24 in. long) circular needle
- US 15 (32 in. long) circular needle
- Two US 15 double-pointed needles
- Knitter's sewing needle or bodkin for sewing
- Large snap (optional)

Finished size

Bag measures approx 9½ in. high by 10½ in. wide.

The fabulous, bright, "jazzy" colors in this bag make it one of my favorites. I love the dreadlock-style fringe that the Elle Pizzazz yarn produces, and this colorway works so well with the turquoise wool yarn I chose for the main body of the bag. The pink eyelash yarn mixed in with the Pizzazz adds color contrast and thickens out the fringe beautifully.

The Pizzazz yarn comes in lots of different color combinations, and I must have knitted versions of this bag using most of them, as they are all so gorgeous.

If you want to try a different color combination to the one I've used here, just choose a wool yarn from the Knitting4fun range that matches one of the strand colors in the Pizzazz. The Ice eyelash yarn is also available in lots of colors, so you can mix-and-match to create your own unique combination.

The book bag version of this pattern (see page 34) will hold lots of paperwork, and is far more stylish than a briefcase. It'll also hold a laptop, and the thick yarn provides extra padding.

Gauge

12 stitches and 14 rows to
4 in. over st st on US 15
needles using two strands of
A held together, although
gauge is not crucial in felting.

Abbreviations

See page 125.

Bag

Using US 11 circular needle and one strand each of A, B, and C held together, cast on 65 sts.

*Join the cast on row into a circle, ensuring that the knitting is not twisted, and place a marker to establish the beginning of the round.

Purl 7 to 9 rounds, or until the trim at the top of the bag is the desired depth. Purling the stitches helps to keep the textured yarn on the right side of the knitting. Tease out the long fibers as you work so that they do not get trapped in the knitted fabric.*

Break off B and C and join in another strand of A.

Next round: [K12, inc] five times. (70 sts)

Change to US 15 circular needle and cont in knit stitch.

Knit 45 rounds using two strands of A held together.

Shape base

Slip marker to the right-hand needle and start the shaping as folls:

Next round: K5, k2tog, k21, k2togtbl, k10, k2tog, k21, k2togtbl, k5. (66 sts)

Next round: K4, k2tog, k21, k2togtbl, k8, k2tog, k21, k2togtbl, k4. (62 sts)

Next round: K3, k2tog, k21, k2togtbl, k6, k2tog, k21, k2togtbl, k3. (58 sts)

Next round: K2, k2tog, k21, k2togtbl, k4, k2tog, k21, k2togtbl, k2. (54 sts)

Next round: K1, k2tog, k21, k2togtbl, k2, k2tog, k21, k2togtbl, k1. (50 sts)

Next round: K2tog, k21, k2togtbl, k2tog, k21, k2togtbl. (46 sts)

**Join base

Turn the bag inside out and push 23 sts along to each needle point. Put both needle points together and, using another knitting needle (the same size as the circular needle or a size larger), knit tog the first st on each needle point. Knit tog the second stitch on each needle point, then slip the first st over the second st, so binding off (not too tightly) and joining the base of the bag at the same time. Rep until all sts are bound off.

Handles (make two)

Using US 15 double-pointed needles and two strands of A held together, cast on 4 sts.

Knit 1 row.

Switch needles in your hands, so the needle with the stitches on is in your left hand again. Slide the stitches to the other end of the needle and, pulling the yarn across the back of the stitches, knit the row again. The first three or four rows will be flat but don't worry, after that the knitting will become tubular. Before knitting the first stitch of each row, give the yarn a tug to make the strand across the back disappear.

Cont in this way, sliding and knitting, until the handle is the required length. As the handles will shrink by approximately one-third during felting, I usually knit about 50–60 rows for a short hand-held handle, 100 rows for a longer hand-held handle, and 120–140 rows for a shoulder handle.

Bind off.

To finish

Using the knitter's sewing needle and A, sew the handles to the inside of the trim section at the top of the bag, about ½ in. down from the top edge.

Darn in all loose ends.

Following the instructions on pages 123–124, machine-wash the bag to felt it.

You can sew on a large snap to fasten the bag if desired.

The Pizzazz yarn comes in lots of different colors, and I must have knitted versions of this bag using most of them, as they are all so gorgeous.

jazzy book bag

You will need

- 14oz of Knitting4fun
  Pure Wool in Turquoise (A)
- 1¾oz of Filati FF Park in
  color 45 (B)
- 7oz of Ice Catena in
  Aqua/Green/Blue (C)

Finished size

Bag measures approx 10½ in.
high by 14 in. wide.

Bag

Using US 11 circular needle and one strand each of A and B held together, cast on 100 sts.

Follow Jazzy Bag pattern from * to *.

Break off B and join in a strand of C.

Next round: [K9, inc] ten times. (110 sts)

Change to US 15 circular needle and cont in knit stitch.

Knit 65 rounds.

Shape base

Slip marker to the right-hand needle and start the shaping as folls:

Next round: K7, k2tog, k41, k2togtbl, k14, k2tog, k41, k2togtbl, k7. (106 sts)

Next round: K6, k2tog, k41, k2togtbl, k12, k2tog, k41, k2togtbl, k6. (102 sts)

Next round: K5, k2tog, k41, k2togtbl, k10, k2tog, k41, k2togtbl, k5. (98 sts)

Next round: K4, k2tog, k41, k2togtbl, k8, k2tog, k41, k2togtbl, k4. (94 sts)

Next round: K3, k2tog, k41, k2togtbl, k6, k2tog, k41, k2togtbl, k3. (90 sts)

Next round: K2, k2tog, k41, k2togtbl, k4, k2tog, k41, k2togtbl, k2. (86 sts)

Next round: K1, k2tog, k41, k2togtbl, k2, k2tog, k41, k2togtbl, k1. (82 sts)

Next round: K2tog, k41, k2togtbl, k2tog, k41, k2togtbl. (78 sts)

Follow Jazzy Bag pattern from **, pushing 39 sts along to each needle point, to complete bag.

orange fluff and bobble

I am a little bobble crazy—I just adore them. The colors in this particular bag were inspired by a jacket I saw in a department store: I loved the gray and burnt orange colors together. This bag is one of many fluff and bobble bags I have made in just about every conceivable color combination.

The Ice Long Eyelash yarn has, as the name suggests, long strands of eyelash and this gives a very thick and luxurious trim to the top of the bag.

I have also made the bag without the eyelash top and just knitted the first few rows at the top in seed stitch to stop the top edge from curling over. The i-cord handles can be made in a variety of lengths to suit your needs.

The three-needle bind off gives a very neat finish, so there is very little sewing up to be done. Once the bag is felted it appears seamless, giving a neat and professional look.

Abbreviations

MB = make bobble: with two strands of contrast color (k1, p1, k1) into next st, turn p3, turn k3, turn p3, turn sk2po, slip the stitch back onto the left-hand needle and knit into it again using main color; cut contrast yarn, pull ends of contrast yarn tight to form the bobble, knot ends together, and sew them into the back of the bobble before felting. Alternatively, strand contrast color on the wrong side between bobbles and cut yarn at the end of each bobble row.

For a smaller bobble, use one strand of color and US 10½ needle to knit the bobble and then return to US 15 needles when knitting the main color.

See also page 125.

Bag

Using US 10½ circular needle and one strand each of A and B held together, cast on 70 sts.

Join the cast on row into a circle, ensuring that the knitting is not twisted, and place a marker to establish the beginning of the round.

Purl 7 to 9 rounds, or until the trim at the top of the bag is the desired depth. Purling the stitches helps to keep the textured yarn on the right side of the knitting. Tease out the long fibers as you work so that they do not get trapped in the knitted fabric.*

Break off B and join in another strand of A.

Next round: [K6, inc] ten times. (80 sts)

Change to US 15 circular needle and cont in knit stitch.

Knit 5 rounds.

Round 6 (bobble round): [K7, MB] to the end of the row.

Knit 7 rounds.

Round 14 (bobble round): K4 [MB, k7] to last 4 sts, MB, k3.

Knit 7 rounds.

Round 22 (bobble round): As round 6.

Knit 7 rounds.

Round 30 (bobble round): As round 14.

Knit 7 rounds.

Round 38 (bobble round): As round 6.

Knit 7 rounds.

Round 46 (bobble round): As round 14.

Knit 5 rounds.

Shape base

Slip marker to the right-hand needle and start the shaping as folls:

Round 52: K5, k2tog, k26, k2togtbl, k10, k2tog, k26, k2togtbl, k5. (76 sts)

Round 53: K4, k2tog, k26, k2togtbl, k8, k2tog, k26, k2togtbl, k4. (72 sts)

Round 54: K3, k2tog, k26, k2togtbl, k6, k2tog, k26, k2togtbl, k3. (68 sts)

Round 55: K2, k2tog, k26, k2togtbl, k4, k2tog, k26, k2togtbl, k2. (64 sts)

Round 56: K1, k2tog, k26, k2togtbl, k2, k2tog, k26, k2togtbl, k1. (60 sts)

Round 57: K2tog, k26, k2togtbl, k2tog, k26, k2togtbl. (56 sts)

Join base

Turn the bag inside out and push 28 sts along to each needle point. Put both needle points together and, using another knitting needle (the same size as the circular needle or a size larger), knit tog the first st on each needle point. Knit tog the second stitch on each needle point, then slip the first st over the second st, so binding off (not too tightly) and joining the base of the bag at the same time. Rep until all sts are bound off.

Handle (make one)

Using US 15 double-pointed needles and two strands of A held together, cast on 4 sts.

Knit 1 row.

Switch needles in your hands, so the needle with the stitches on is in your left hand again. Slide the stitches to the other end of the needle and, pulling the yarn across the back of the stitches, knit the row again. The first three or four rows will be flat but don't worry, after that the knitting will become tubular. Before knitting the first stitch of each row, give the yarn a tug to make the strand across the back disappear.

Cont in this way, sliding and knitting, until the handle is the required length. As the handles will shrink by approximately one-third during felting, I usually knit about 50–60 rows for a short hand-held handle, 100 rows for a longer hand-held handle, and 120–140 rows for a shoulder handle.

Bind off.

To finish

Using the knitter's sewing needle and A, sew the handle to the inside of the trim section at the top of the bag, about ½ in. down from the top edge.

Darn in all loose ends.

Following the instructions on pages 123–124, machine-wash the bag to felt it.

You can sew on a large snap to fasten the bag if desired.

red fluff and bobble

This dramatic bag is knitted following the same pattern as Orange Fluff And Bobble, but using black wool for the main color with red bobbles and top trim.

This bag is one of many fluff and bobble bags I have made in just about every conceivable color combo.

anything goes stash bag

You will need
- 7oz of Knitting4fun Pure Merino Wool (A)
- Small amounts of eyelash, feather, and other fancy yarns
- US 11 (16 in. or 24 in. long) circular needle
- US 15 (24 in. long) circular needle
- Knitter's sewing needle or bodkin for sewing
- Large snap (optional)

Finished size
Bag measures approx 8 in. high by 8 in. wide.

Gauge
12 stitches and 14 rows to 4 in. over st st on US 15 needles using two strands of A held together, although gauge is not crucial in felting.

What do you do with all the bits of yarns that you have lying around? I had lots of eyelash yarns, feather yarns, ribbon yarns, and other fancy types, and just wanted to use up some of these small bits. This "bitsa" bag was my answer; "with bits of this and bits of that" it's a great stash buster. I have used Turquoise and Fuchsia Knitting4fun yarns as those colors worked perfectly with the fancy yarns I had.

The bag is knitted in pure wool and the other yarns are added in randomly throughout to create texture, using slip stitches, bobbles, and other stitch patterns. Anything goes and your imagination is the only limit. You can achieve wonderful textures by just adding a fancy yarn to one strand of the wool and knitting them together. You do not have to knit a complete row in each chosen yarn—they can be very random.

The ends of the yarns can be left hanging out if you do not want to sew or weave them in. This gives great added texture, resembling tassels and fringes. An i-cord handle completes the bag, which can then be embellished further with textured yarns or with buttons and beads.

rounded stash bag

Work as for Anything Goes Stash Bag from * to *.

Shape base

Slip marker to the right-hand needle and start the shaping as folls:

Next round: [K8, k2tog] to the end of the round. (54 sts)

Knit 2 rounds.

Next round: [K7, k2tog] to the end of the round. (48 sts)

Knit 1 round.

Change to US 15 double-pointed needles as folls:

Next round: *[K6, k2tog] twice onto one double-pointed needle; rep from * onto two more needles. (42 sts)

Cont shaping on double-pointed needles as folls:

Knit 1 round.

Next round: [K5, k2tog] to the end of the round. (36 sts)

Next round: [K4, k2tog] to the end of the round. (30 sts)

Next round: [K3, k2tog] to the end of the round. (24 sts)

Next round: [K2, k2tog] to the end of the round. (18 sts)

Next round: [K1, k2tog] to the end of the round. (12 sts)

Next round: [K2tog] to the end of the round. (6 sts)

Leaving a 15 in. tail, cut yarn. Thread tail through rem sts. Thread tail into knitter's sewing needle and sew through these sts several times to secure the end.

Make handle and finish as for Anything Goes Stash Bag.

retro button bag

I have fond memories of sorting through my grandmother's button box and I eventually inherited some of the wonderful buttons. What do you do with all of these buttons, especially the precious ones with memories attached? It seems a shame to have them hidden away in tins, boxes, and drawers. I decided to use them on my bags and I have decorated many bags with buttons old and new.

The buttons can be layered, which means that some of the less interesting ones can be stacked to give depth and add color. So use up your button stash and enjoy them, after all you can always cut them off again and use them on something else when you have had enough of that particular bag.

I sew the buttons on after felting, as the first time I made one of these bags I planned the positions of the buttons, taking about three hours to sew them on, carefully spacing them, and arranging the colors, forgetting that when the bag was felted, the positions would move. I had to cut some buttons off and change the positions to get a better effect.

Gauge

12 stitches and 14 rows to
4 in. over st st on US 15
needles using two strands of
A held together, although
gauge is not crucial in felting.

Abbreviations

See page 125.

Bag

Using US 11 circular needle and one strand each of A and B held together, cast on
65 sts.

Join the cast on row into a circle, ensuring that the knitting is not twisted, and
place a marker to establish the beginning of the round.

Purl 8 rounds, or until the trim at the top of the bag is the desired depth. Purling
the stitches helps to keep the textured yarn on the right side of the knitting. Tease
out the long fibers as you work so that they do not get trapped in the knitted fabric.

Break off B and join in another strand of A.

Round 9: [K12, inc] five times. (70 sts)

Change to US 15 circular needle and cont in knit stitch.

Knit 45 rounds using two strands of A held together.

Shape base

Slip marker to the right-hand needle and start the shaping as folls:

Round 55: K5, k2tog, k21, k2togtbl, k10, k2tog, k21, k2togtbl, k5. (66 sts)

Round 56: K4, k2tog, k21, k2togtbl, k8, k2tog, k21, k2togtbl, k4. (62 sts)

Round 57: K3, k2tog, k21, k2togtbl, k6, k2tog, k21, k2togtbl, k3. (58 sts)

Round 58: K2, k2tog, k21, k2togtbl, k4, k2tog, k21, k2togtbl, k2. (54 sts)

Round 59: K1, k2tog, k21, k2togtbl, k2, k2tog, k21, k2togtbl, k1. (50 sts)

Round 60: K2tog, k21, k2togtbl, k2tog, k21, k2togtbl. (46 sts)

Join base

Turn the bag inside out and push 23 sts along to each needle point. Put both needle
points together and, using another knitting needle (the same size as the circular
needle or a size larger), knit tog the first st on each needle point. Knit tog the second
stitch on each needle point, then slip the first st over the second st, so binding off
(not too tightly) and joining the base of the bag at the same time. Rep until all sts are
bound off.

Handles (make two)

Using US 15 double-pointed needles and two strands of A held together, cast on
4 sts.

Knit 1 row.

Switch needles in your hands, so the needle with the stitches on is in your left hand
again. Slide the stitches to the other end of the needle and, pulling the yarn across
the back of the stitches, knit the row again. The first three or four rows will be flat but

don't worry, after that the knitting will become tubular. Before knitting the first stitch of each row, give the yarn a tug to make the strand across the back disappear.

Cont in this way, sliding and knitting, until the handle is the required length. As the handles will shrink by approximately one-third during felting, I usually knit about 50–60 rows for a short hand-held handle, 100 rows for a longer hand-held handle, and 120–140 rows for a shoulder handle.

Bind off.

To finish

Using the knitter's sewing needle and A, sew the handles to the inside of the trim section at the top of the bag, about ½ in. down from the top edge.

Darn in all loose ends.

Following the instructions on pages 123–124, machine-wash the bag to felt it.

Using the sewing needle and thread, sew the decorative buttons onto the felted bag. Stack two or three on top of one another or sew them on singly, as preferred.

You can sew on a large snap to fasten the bag if desired.

What do you do with all your buttons, especially the precious ones with memories attached? It seems a shame to have them hidden away in tins, boxes, and drawers.

slip stitch honeycomb

You will need

- 5¼oz of Knitting4fun Pure Wool in Fuchsia (A)
- 1¾oz of Ice Long Eyelash in each of Fuchsia 4112 and Orange 8814 (B and C)
- 5¼oz of Knitting4fun Pure Wool in Orange (D)
- US 11 (24 in. long) circular needle
- US 15 (24 in. or 32 in. long) circular needle
- Pair of US 11 knitting needles
- Pair of plastic bag handles
- Knitter's sewing needle or bodkin for sewing
- Large snap (optional)

Finished size

Bag measures approx 10 in. high by 10½ in. wide.

This bag was inspired by the outfit of a young Asian girl I met in Goa, India. The hot pink and orange colors of her sari just shone in the sunlight and I decided to make this bag in similar colors to keep that great memory alive.

The bag is knitted in a slip stitch design to create a honeycomb effect. I have used two different colors of Ice Long Eyelash yarn for the top edge so that I could mix pink and orange, giving a thick top with the two vivid colors shaded together.

The orange plastic handles complement the design and the colorway perfectly, though you could make i-cord handles if you prefer, like those on Pure Purple (see page 10).

This bag can be made in any color combination to match any outfit. Alternatively, you can knit the honeycomb rows in a variety of different colors to create a stained-glass window effect.

shaped
bags

With shaping at the top edge and around the base, these bags are elegant-looking as well as useful accessories. Carry one on casual jeans days or smart suit days and it'll look equally good.

red wool and ribbon

You will need

- 3½oz of Knitting4fun Pure Wool in Red (A)
- 3½oz of Colinette Giotto in Fire 71 (B)
- US 11 (24 in. long) circular needle
- US 15 (24 in. long) circular needle
- Two US 15 double-pointed needles
- Pair of US 11 knitting needles
- Knitter's sewing needle or bodkin for sewing
- Decorative flower-shaped button
- Sewing needle and thread
- Large snap (optional)

Finished size

Bag measures approx 7 in. high by 9 in. wide.

This dainty bag was made for a friend's teenage daughter who was going to a summer garden party. I chose the red wool color to match the dress she was planning to wear.

The lovely variegated colors in the hand-dyed Colinette Giotto ribbon yarn are so exciting and they complement the red wool beautifully. When the bag is felted, the ribbon yarn produces a tweedy effect with a sheen that I just adore.

The ribbon flower is stitched to a brooch back so that it can be worn pinned to a dress or jacket, or just left on the bag. For a thoroughly coordinated look, make two flowers—one to embellish the bag and one to be worn as a corsage.

Gauge

12 stitches and 14 rows to
4 in. over st st on US 15
needles using one strand
each of A and B held
together, although gauge is
not crucial in felting.

Abbreviations

See page 125.

Bag

Using US 11 circular needle and one strand each of A and B held together, cast on
65 sts.

Join the cast on row into a circle, ensuring that the knitting is not twisted, and
place a marker to establish the beginning of the round.

Round 1: [K1, p1] to last st, k1.

Round 2: [P1, k1] to last st, p1.

Rep rounds 1–2 once more then rep round 1 once more.

Round 6: [K12, inc] five times. (70 sts)

Change to US 15 circular needle and cont in knit stitch.

Knit 10 rounds.

Shape sides

Slip marker to the right-hand needle and start the shaping as folls:

Round 17: K3, M1, k29, M1, k6, M1, k29, M1, k3. (74 sts)

Knit 10 rounds.

Round 28: K4, M1, k29, M1, k8, M1, k29, M1, k4. (78 sts)

Knit 10 rounds.

Round 39: K5, M1, k29, M1, k10, M1, k29, M1, k5. (82 sts)

Knit 15 rounds.

Shape base

Slip marker to the right-hand needle and start the shaping as folls:

Round 55: K5, k2tog, k27, k2togtbl, k10, k2tog, k27, k2togtbl, k5. (78 sts)

Round 56: K4, k2tog, k27, k2togtbl, k8, k2tog, k27, k2togtbl, k4. (74 sts)

Round 57: K3, k2tog, k27, k2togtbl, k6, k2tog, k27, k2togtbl, k3. (70 sts)

Round 58: K2, k2tog, k27, k2togtbl, k4, k2tog, k27, k2togtbl, k2. (66 sts)

Round 59: K1, k2tog, k27, k2togtbl, k2, k2tog, k27, k2togtbl, k1. (62 sts)

Round 60: K2tog, k27, k2togtbl, k2tog, k27, k2togtbl. (58 sts)

Join base

Turn the bag inside out and push 29 sts along to each needle point. Put both needle
points together and, using another knitting needle (the same size as the circular
needle or a size larger), knit tog the first st on each needle point. Knit tog the second
stitch on each needle point, then slip the first st over the second st, so binding off
(not too tightly) and joining the base of the bag at the same time. Rep until all sts are
bound off.

Flower

Using US 11 needles and one strand of B, cast on 63 sts.

Row 1 (RS): Knit.

Row 2: P1, p2tog, p1, p2togtbl, *p3, p2tog, p1, p2togtbl; rep from * to last st, p1. (47 sts)

Row 3: *Skpo, k1, k2tog, k1; rep from * to last 5 sts, skpo, k1, k2tog. (31 sts)

Row 4: P3tog *p1, p3tog; rep from * to the end of the row. (15 sts)

Row 5: Sk2po *k1, sk2po; rep from * to the end of the row. (7 sts)

Leaving a 15 in. tail, cut yarn. Thread tail through rem sts and pull up tightly. Thread tail into knitter's sewing needle and join seam to complete flower.

Handles (make two)

Using US 15 double-pointed needles and two strands of A held together, cast on 3 sts.

Knit 1 row.

Switch needles in your hands, so the needle with the stitches on is in your left hand again. Slide the stitches to the other end of the needle and, pulling the yarn across the back of the stitches, knit the row again. The first three or four rows will be flat but don't worry, after that the knitting will become tubular. Before knitting the first stitch of each row, give the yarn a tug to make the strand across the back disappear.

Cont in this way, sliding and knitting, until the handle is the required length. As the handles will shrink by approximately one-third during felting, I usually knit about 50–60 rows for a short hand-held handle, 100 rows for a longer hand-held handle, and 120–140 rows for a shoulder handle.

Bind off.

To finish

Using the knitter's sewing needle and A, sew the handles to the inside of the trim section at the top of the bag, about ½ in. down from the top edge.

Using the knitter's sewing needle and A, sew the flower to the front of the bag.

Darn in all loose ends.

Following the instructions on pages 123–124, machine-wash the bag to felt it.

Using the sewing needle and thread, sew the button to the center of the flower.

You can sew on a large snap to fasten the bag if desired.

The lovely variegated colors in the hand-dyed Colinette Giotto ribbon yarn are so exciting and they complement the red wool beautifully.

cherry ripe

You will need

- 4½oz of Knitting4fun Natural Merino Wool in Dark Gray (A)
- 4½oz of Knitting4fun Natural Merino Wool in Light Gray (B)
- ¾oz of Knitting4fun Space-dyed Pure Wool in Red (C)
- ¾oz of Knitting4fun Space-dyed Pure Wool in Green (D)
- US 11 (16 in. or 24 in. long) circular needle
- US 15 (24 in. or 32 in. long) circular needle
- Pair of US 11 knitting needles
- Pair of plastic bag handles
- Knitter's sewing needle or bodkin for sewing
- Small amount of stuffing
- Large snap (optional)

Finished size

Bag measures approx 9 in. high by 11½ in. wide.

Having seen some beautiful, ripe, shiny cherries while visiting a market, I decided to make a cherry bag that was fun and funky. The cherries are knitted using red space-dyed yarn to give them a really ripe, fresh look. Each cherry is a small knitted bobble that is stuffed using some wool tops or some toy stuffing.

To give the leaves some shading they are knitted in green space-dyed yarn The subtly variegated colors of these space-dyed yarns work really well for knitting flowers, leaves, and berries—anything natural in fact.

Once the leaves and cherries are complete, they are stitched together into a bunch and sewn onto the bag. If you love these perky fruit motifs, then you can knit more of them and make the Bunch of Cherries bag on page 64.

Gauge

12 stitches and 14 rows to 4 in. over st st on US 15 needles using one strand each of A and B held together, although gauge is not crucial in felting.

Abbreviations

See page 125.

Bag

Using US 11 circular needle and one strand each of A and B held together, cast on 75 sts.

Join the cast on row into a circle, ensuring that the knitting is not twisted, and place a marker to establish the beginning of the round.

Round 1: [K1, p1] to last st, k1.

Round 2: [P1, k1] to last st, p1.

Rep rounds 1–2 twice more.

Round 7: [K14, inc] five times. (80 sts)

Change to US 15 circular needle and cont in knit stitch.

Knit 10 rounds.

Shape sides

Slip marker to the right-hand needle and start the shaping as folls:

Round 18: K4, M1, k32, M1, k8, M1, k32, M1, k4. (84 sts)

Knit 10 rounds.

Round 29: K5, M1, k32, M1, k10, M1, k32, M1, k5. (88 sts)

Knit 10 rounds.

Round 40: K6, M1, k32, M1, k12, M1, k32, M1, k6. (92 sts)

Knit 15 rounds.

Shape base

Slip marker to the right-hand needle and start the shaping as folls:

Round 56: K6, k2tog, k30, k2togtbl, k12, k2tog, k30, k2togtbl, k6. (88 sts)

Round 57: K5, k2tog, k30, k2togtbl, k10, k2tog, k30, k2togtbl, k5. (84 sts)

Round 58: K4, k2tog, k30, k2togtbl, k8, k2tog, k30, k2togtbl, k4. (80 sts)

Round 59: K3, k2tog, k30, k2togtbl, k6, k2tog, k30, k2togtbl, k3. (76 sts)

Round 60: K2, k2tog, k30, k2togtbl, k4, k2tog, k30, k2togtbl, k2. (72 sts)

Round 61: K1, k2tog, k30, k2togtbl, k2, k2tog, k30, k2togtbl, k1. (68 sts)

Round 62: K2tog, k30, k2togtbl, k2tog, k30, k2togtbl. (64 sts)

Join base

Turn the bag inside out and push 32 sts along to each needle point. Put both needle points together and, using another knitting needle (the same size as the circular needle or a size larger), knit tog the first st on each needle point. Knit tog the second stitch on each needle point, then slip the first st over the second st, so binding off (not too tightly) and joining the base of the bag at the same time. Rep until all sts are bound off.

Handle tabs (make four)

Using US 11 needles and one strand of A, cast on 4 sts.

Knit 8 rows.

Bind off.

Cherry (make three)

Using US 11 needles and one strand of C, cast on 3 sts.

Row 1 (RS): Inc in each stitch. (6 sts)

Starting with a purl row, work 5 rows st st.

Row 7: [K2tog] 3 times. (3 sts)

Row 8: Sl1, p2tog, psso.

Leaving a 20 in. tail, cut yarn and fasten off.

Thread knitter's sewing needle or bodkin with tail and sew side seam to form a large bobble, stuffing bobble lightly as you sew. Darn in the end.

Leaf (make three)

Using US 11 needles and one strand of D, cast on 3 sts.

Row 1 (RS): Knit.

Row 2 and all alt rows: Purl.

Row 3: K1, M1, k1, M1, k1. (5 sts)

Row 5: K1, M1, k3, M1, k1. (7 sts)

Rows 7 and 9: Knit.

Row 11: K1, k2tog, k1, k2tog, k1. (5 sts)

Row 13: K2tog, k1, k2tog. (3 sts)

Row 14: Sl1, p2tog, psso.

Leaving a 20 in. tail, cut yarn and fasten off.

To finish

Using tails of yarn, the knitter's sewing needle or bodkin, and following photograph for position, sew leaves in a group to front of bag.

Thread a double strand of D through the top of each cherry and sew them on to the bag below the leaves, leaving about 3 in. of green yarn free above the cherry for the stalk. The strands will join together during the felting process to make a single, slim stalk. Alternatively, join D to the cherry and crochet a 3 in. chain before sewing the cherry to the bag.

The subtly variegated colors of these space-dyed yarns work really well for knitting flowers, leaves, and berries.

Measure the space between the slots in the bag handles and mark the positions with pins on the inside of the top of the bag. Thread the knitter's sewing needle or bodkin with one strand of A and sew one narrow end of a strip to each marked point, about ¼ in. down from the top edge. Thread the strips through the slots in the plastic handles. Sew the other narrow end of each strip to the inside of the bag, about ¼ in. below the first end.

Wrap the plastic handles tightly in bubble wrap and, with the bag right side out, fold the handles into the inside of the bag; this will protect them during the felting process in the washing machine. Close the bag opening with a safety pin or something similar to stop the handles from falling out.

If you want to use a wooden, beaded, or bamboo handle that cannot be put through the wash cycle, then sew one end of each strip in place as described. Felt the bag, then thread the felted strips through the slots and sew the free ends in place.

Darn in all loose ends.

Following the instructions on pages 123–124, machine-wash the bag to felt it.

You can sew on a large snap to fasten the bag if desired.

bunch of cherries

This bag is made following the same pattern as Cherry Ripe, but using two strands of Knitting4fun Pure Wool in Black. Twelve cherries and twelve leaves are made and sewn in groups of two around the top edge (front and back) of the bag.

recycled sari silk bag

You will need

- 4oz of Knitting4fun Pure Wool in Fuchsia (A)
- 10½oz of Knitting4fun Recycled Sari Silk Yarn (B)
- Small amounts of Knitting4fun Pure Wool for flowers and leaves
- US 11 (16 in. or 24 in. long) circular needle
- US 15 (32 in. long) circular needle
- Pair of US 11 knitting needles
- Pair of plastic bag handles
- Knitter's sewing needle or bodkin for sewing
- Decorative beads (optional)
- Large snap (optional)

Finished size

Bag measures approx 9 in. high by 13 in. wide.

I have collected many different skeins of recycled sari silk yarns in wonderful jewel-like colors, but what do you do with all of them? I keep them in glass vases just to look at, but I did want to try to use some of them in a bag.

For this design I knitted one strand of pure wool and one strand of the sari silk yarn together. As the sari silk is hand-spun and every skein is different, I had to knit from two balls at the same time, alternating them on each row so that the colors blended well. Once felted, the sari silk is trapped by the wool, leaving a textured surface with lots of jewel colors popping through the main color.

I made different flowers to decorate the bag—larger ones, clusters of small ones, and leaves or corkscrew leaf tendrils. I sewed some to brooch backs, so that they can be removed and the decorations can be changed.

In Nepal I found some banana fiber yarn with similar random colors, but a little more sheen than the sari silk yarn. I made the purple bag on page 70 from this yarn—it doesn't smell of bananas though!

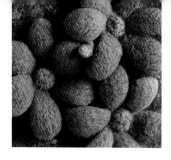

banana fiber bag

Swap the recycled sari yarn for banana fiber then follow the same pattern to make this bag. The flower and leaves are made using the following patterns.

Large flower

Using one strand of pure wool and US 11 knitting needles, cast on 15 sts.

Row 1: K14, turn.

Row 2: Sl1, k12, turn.

Row 3: Sl1, k11, turn.

Row 4: Sl1, k10, turn.

Cont as set, slipping 1 st and knitting 9, 8, 7, 6, 5, 4, 3 sts on consecutive rows.

Row 12: Sl1, knit to the end of the row.

Row 13: Skpo, then bind off all sts.

Leave rem st on needle and cast on 10 more sts. (11 sts)

Rep rows 1–13 four or five times more to give five or six petals, as desired.

Leaving a 20 in. tail, cut yarn. Thread knitter's sewing needle or bodkin with tail and sew through the edge of each petal and gather up, pulling the petals into a ring. Sew through the center to hold the flower together. This pattern makes the pink flower shown opposite. To make the smaller flowers shown above left, cast on 11 sts and follow the large flower pattern on page 99.

Flower center

Using US 11 needles and one strand of pure fine wool, cast on 3 sts.

Row 1 (RS): Inc in each stitch. (6 sts)

Starting with a purl row, work 5 rows st st.

Row 7: [K2tog] 3 times. (3 sts)

Row 8: Sl1, p2tog, psso.

Leaving a 20 in. tail, cut yarn and fasten off.

Thread knitter's sewing needle or bodkin with tail and sew side seam to form a large bobble, stuffing bobble lightly as you sew. Darn in the end.

Corkscrew leaf

Using US 11 knitting needles and one strand of fine pure wool, cast on 40 sts.

Row 1: [K2tog] to the end of the row. (20 sts)

Row 2: [K2tog] to the end of the row. (10 sts)

Bind off.

Make 2 or 3 leaves; you can vary the size by casting on more or fewer stitches.

Using the tails of yarn and following the photograph for position, sew the leaves to the bag. Sew the flower center into the petals and sew the flower to the bag.

little saddle bag

You will need
- 7oz of Knitting4fun Pure Wool in Deep Pink (A)
- 7oz of Lang Mille Colori in color 65 (B)
- US 11 (32 in. long) circular needle
- US 15 (32 in. long) circular needle
- Pair of US 11 knitting needles
- Pair of US 15 knitting needles
- Knitter's sewing needle or bodkin for sewing
- Button or toggle for fastening

Finished size
Bag measures approx 7½ in. high by 8½ in. wide.

I found myself having to use crutches for a while and suddenly realized how hard it is to carry things while using crutches. I had always made my bags with shorter handles, but now I needed a bag that I could wear across my body, leaving my hands free.

I made this bag from a pure wool yarn and a random-dyed yarn that is 50 percent super-wash wool and 50 percent acrylic, which when felted gives a lovely bouclé effect.

I used seed stitch for the strap so that it stayed flat and was comfortable to wear. As my hands were occupied (by the crutches) I also needed extra security, so this bag has a flap with a button closure. The button was stitched on with the pure wool so that it felted into position, making it a strong fastening.

This style of bag can be made in any size: larger sizes are great for laptops and smaller sizes are ideal for carrying bottles of water—you can't carry mugs of tea when you are on crutches!

Gauge

12 stitches and 14 rows to 4 in. over st st on US 15 needles using one strand each of A and B held together, although gauge is not crucial in felting.

Abbreviations

See page 125.

Bag

Using US 11 circular needle and one strand each of A and B held together, cast on 75 sts.

Join the cast on row into a circle, ensuring that the knitting is not twisted, and place a marker to establish the beginning of the round.

Round 1: [K1, p1] to last st, k1.

Round 2: [P1, k1] to last st, p1.

Rep rounds 1–2 twice more.

Round 7: [K14, inc] five times. (80 sts)

Change to US 15 circular needle and cont in knit stitch.

Knit 10 rounds.

Shape sides

Slip marker to the right-hand needle and start the shaping as folls:

Round 18: K4, M1, k32, M1, k8, M1, k32, M1, k4. (84 sts)

Knit 10 rounds.

Round 29: K5, M1, k32, M1, k10, M1, k32, M1, k5. (88 sts)

Knit 10 rounds.

Round 40: K6, M1, k32, M1, k12, M1, k32, M1, k6. (92 sts)

Knit 25 rounds.

Shape base

Slip marker to the right-hand needle and start the shaping as folls:

Round 66: K6, k2tog, k30, k2togtbl, k12, k2tog, k30, k2togtbl, k6. (88 sts)

Round 67: K5, k2tog, k30, k2togtbl, k10, k2tog, k30, k2togtbl, k5. (84 sts)

Round 68: K4, k2tog, k30, k2togtbl, k8, k2tog, k30, k2togtbl, k4. (80 sts)

Round 69: K3, k2tog, k30, k2togtbl, k6, k2tog, k30, k2togtbl, k3. (76 sts)

Round 70: K2, k2tog, k30, k2togtbl, k4, k2tog, k30, k2togtbl, k2. (72 sts)

Round 71: K1, k2tog, k30, k2togtbl, k2, k2tog, k30, k2togtbl, k1. (68 sts)

Round 72: K2tog, k30, k2togtbl, k2tog, k30, k2togtbl. (64 sts)

Join base

Turn the bag inside out and push 32 sts along to each needle point. Put both needle points together and, using another knitting needle (the same size as the circular needle or a size larger), knit tog the first st on each needle point. Knit tog the second stitch on each needle point, then slip the first st over the second st, so binding off (not too tightly) and joining the base of the bag at the same time. Rep until all sts are bound off.

Flap

Lay the bag flat with the bound-off seam running along the bottom. In line with the first increase made in round 18, place a pin in the top edge of the back of the bag. On the same edge, place a second pin in line with the second increase.

With the right side facing, one strand each of A and B held together, and US 11 knitting needles, pick up 33 sts between the pins.

Row 1: [K1, p1] to last st, k1.

Row 2: As row 1.

Change to US 15 knitting needles.

Rep row 1 ten more times.

Row 13: Inc, [p1, k1] to last 2 sts, p1, inc. (35 sts)

Row 14: [P1, k1] to last st, p1.

Rep row 14 nine more times.

Row 24: Inc [k1, p1] to last 2 sts, k1, inc. (37 sts)

Row 25: [K1, p1] to last st, k1.

Rep row 25 nine more times.

Row 35: K2togtbl, [k1, p1] to last 2 sts, k2tog. (35 sts)

Keeping seed st patt correct, rep row 35 four more times. (27 sts)

Row 40 (1st buttonhole row): K2togtbl, seed 10, bind off 3 sts, seed to last 2 sts, k2tog.

Row 41 (2nd buttonhole row): Seed 11, cast on 3 sts, seed 11. (25 sts)

Row 42: K2togtbl, seed to last 2 sts, k2tog. (23 sts)

Keeping seed st patt correct, rep row 42 three more times. (17 sts)

Bind off.

Handle

Using US 11 knitting needles and one strand of A, pick up 5 sts along the top edge of the bag at one side of the flap.

Row 1: K1, p1, k1, p1, k1.

Rep row 1 until handle measures 48 in. long.

Bind off.

To finish

Using the knitter's sewing needle and A, sew the free end of the handle to the opposite top edge of the bag.

Darn in all loose ends.

Following the instructions on pages 123–124, machine-wash the bag to felt it.

Sew the toggle to the front of the bag to align with the buttonhole in the flap.

I made this bag from a pure wool yarn and a random-dyed yarn that is 50 percent super-wash wool and 50 percent acrylic, which when felted gives a lovely bouclé effect.

acorn and oak leaf

You will need

- 5¼oz of Knitting4fun Pure Wool in Apple Green (A)
- 4½oz of Noro Kureyon in 201 (B)
- Small amounts of Knitting4fun Pure Wool in Gold (C) and Brown (D)
- Small amount of Knitting4fun Space-dyed Pure Wool in Green (E)
- US 11 (24 in. long) circular needle
- US 15 (32 in. long) circular needle
- Pair of US 11 knitting needles
- Pair of plastic bag handles
- Knitter's sewing needle or bodkin for sewing
- Small amount of stuffing
- Large snap (optional)

Finished size

Bag measures approx 9½ in. high by 11½ in. wide.

This is my Sherwood Forest bag. I live in Nottingham, England, the home of Robin Hood, where legend has it that Robin lived with his band of outlaws among the mighty oaks in the depths of Sherwood Forest. There are many films that tell the story. (The idea of men in tights is still something I find a little worrying!)

This bag is knitted with Noro Kureyon yarn and a pure wool yarn held together to give the variegated colors of the forest in the Fall. Using small amounts of gold and brown pure wool for the acorns and space-dyed green pure wool for the leaves gives them a suitably naturalistic look.

The oak leaves and acorns that decorate the bag can be stitched on or they can be sewn to a brooch back so that they can be removed. A dark brown plastic handle completes the design.

Row 25: Knit.
Row 26: K2togtbl, k3, k2tog. (5 sts)
Row 27: K2togtbl, k1, k2tog. (3 sts)
Row 28: Sk2po.
Cut yarn and fasten off. Darn in end.

To finish

Using tails of yarn and following the photograph for position, sew leaves in a group to front of bag.

Thread a double strand of D through the top of each acorn and sew them below the leaves, leaving about 2½ in. of brown yarn free above the acorn for the stalk. Alternatively, join D to the acorn and crochet a 2½ in. chain before sewing the acorn to the bag.

Measure the space between the slots in the bag handles and mark the positions with pins on the inside of the top of the bag. Thread the knitter's sewing needle or bodkin with one strand of A and sew one narrow end of a strip to each marked point, about ¼ in. down from the top edge. Thread the strips through the slots in the plastic handles. Sew the other narrow end of each strip to the inside of the bag, about ¼ in. below the first end.

Wrap the plastic handles tightly in bubble wrap and, with the bag right side out, fold the handles into the inside of the bag; this will protect them during the felting process in the washing machine. Close the bag opening with a safety pin or something similar to stop the handles from falling out.

If you want to use a wooden, beaded, or bamboo handle that cannot be put through the wash cycle, then sew one end of each strip in place as described. Felt the bag, then thread the felted strips through the slots and sew the free ends in place.

Darn in all loose ends.

Following the instructions on pages 123–124, machine-wash the bag to felt it.

You can sew on a large snap to fasten the bag if desired.

monochrome jazz

You will need

- 8¾oz of Knitting4fun Pure Wool in Black (A)
- 1¾oz of Elle Pizzazz in Zest 250 (B)
- 1¾oz of Ice Long Eyelash in Black 7711 (C)
- US 11 (16 in. or 24 in. long) circular needle
- US 15 (24 in. or 32 in. long) circular needle
- Pair of US 11 knitting needles
- Pair of plastic bag handles
- Knitter's sewing needle or bodkin for sewing
- Large snap (optional)

Finished size

Bag measures approx 9½ in. high by 11½ in. wide.
See page 125.

Being a color fiend, black and white is an unusual combination for me, but it is very striking. I made this bag when I had an important business meeting to go to. As I had to wear a suit, I wanted my bag to be extra-funky so that I didn't look too formal.

The Elle Pizzazz yarn comes in a black and white colorway, so it was perfect for what I wanted. I added in a black eyelash yarn, too, and knitted the two fancy yarns together with the black wool yarn to make a wonderful textured trim for this stylish bag.

The black and white plastic handles do look good, but the bag also looks great with plain black handles or knitted i-cord ones.

Gauge

12 stitches and 14 rows to
4 in. over st st on US 15
needles using two strands of
A held together, although
gauge is not crucial in felting.

Abbreviations

See page 125.

Bag

Using US 11 circular needle and one strand each of A, B, and C held together, cast on 75 sts.

Join the cast on row into a circle, ensuring that the knitting is not twisted, and place a marker to establish the beginning of the round.

Purl 8 rounds, or until the trim at the top of the bag is the desired depth. Purling the stitches helps to keep the textured yarn on the right side of the knitting. Tease out the long fibers as you work so that they do not get trapped in the knitted fabric.

Cut B and C and join in another strand of A.

Round 9: [K14, inc] five times. (80 sts)

Change to US 15 circular needle.

Knit 10 rounds.

Shape sides

Slip marker to the right-hand needle and start the shaping as folls:

Round 20: K4, M1, k32, M1, k8, M1, k32, M1, k4. (84 sts)

Knit 10 rounds.

Round 31: K5, M1, k32, M1, k10, M1, k32, M1, k5. (88 sts)

Knit 10 rounds.

Round 42: K6, M1, k32, M1, k12, M1, k32, M1, k6. (92 sts)

Knit 15 rounds.

Shape base

Slip marker to the right-hand needle and start the shaping as folls:

Round 58: K6, k2tog, k30, k2togtbl, k12, k2tog, k30, k2togtbl, k6. (88 sts)

Round 59: K5, k2tog, k30, k2togtbl, k10, k2tog, k30, k2togtbl, k5. (84 sts)

Round 60: K4, k2tog, k30, k2togtbl, k8, k2tog, k30, k2togtbl, k4. (80 sts)

Round 61: K3, k2tog, k30, k2togtbl, k6, k2tog, k30, k2togtbl, k3. (76 sts)

Round 62: K2, k2tog, k30, k2togtbl, k4, k2tog, k30, k2togtbl, k2. (72 sts)

Round 63: K1, k2tog, k30, k2togtbl, k2, k2tog, k30, k2togtbl, k1. (68 sts)

Round 64: K2tog, k30, k2togtbl, k2tog, k30, k2togtbl. (64 sts)

Join base

Turn the bag inside out and push 32 sts along to each needle point. Put both needle points together and, using another knitting needle (the same size as the circular needle or a size larger), knit tog the first st on each needle point. Knit tog the second stitch on each needle point, then slip the first st over the second st, so binding off (not too tightly)z and joining the base of the bag at the same time. Rep until all sts are bound off.

Handle tabs (make four)
Using US 11 needles and one strand of A, cast on 4 sts.
Knit 10 rows.
Bind off.

To finish
Measure the space between the slots in the bag handles and mark the positions with pins on the inside of the top of the bag. Thread the knitter's sewing needle or bodkin with one strand of A and sew one narrow end of a strip to each marked point, about ¼ in. down from the top edge. Thread the strips through the slots in the plastic handles. Sew the other narrow end of each strip to the inside of the bag, about ¼ in. below the first end.

Wrap the plastic handles tightly in bubble wrap and, with the bag right side out, fold the handles into the inside of the bag; this will protect them during the felting process in the washing machine. Close the bag opening with a safety pin or something similar to stop the handles from falling out.

If you want to use a wooden, beaded, or bamboo handle that cannot be put through the wash cycle, then sew one end of each strip in place as described. Felt the bag, then thread the felted strips through the slots and sew the free ends in place.

Darn in all loose ends.

Following the instructions on pages 123–124, machine-wash the bag to felt it.

You can sew on a large snap to fasten the bag if desired.

I made this bag when I had an important business meeting to go to. As I had to wear a suit, I wanted my bag to be extra-funky so that I didn't look too formal.

variegated stripe bag

You will need

- 3½oz of Knitting4fun Pure Wool in Jade Blue (A)
- 3½oz of Noro Kureyon in 173 (B)
- Small amounts of pure wool or mohair for flowers and leaves
- US 11 (16 in. or 24 in. long) circular needle
- US 15 (32 in. long) circular needle
- Pair of US 11 knitting needles
- Pair of plastic bag handles
- Knitter's sewing needle or bodkin for sewing
- Large snap (optional)
- Decorative beads (optional)

Finished size

Bag measures approx 9 in. high by 11½ in. wide.

This has to be one of my favorite bags and is inspired by the wonderful colors available in the Japanese Noro Kureyon yarn. I have knitted so many bags using almost every shade of this yarn.

The Noro Kureyon yarn knits up to give a striped effect, so for this bag I blended it with one strand of pure wool yarn to get a more subtle variegated effect. The mix of yarns also gives a firmer felt than the Noro yarn gives when used alone.

These bags can be decorated with flowers—large ones, small ones, or clusters of either or both. Alternatively they can have no extra decoration at all; just enjoy the gorgeous colors of the blended yarns.

Using different-colored plastic handles to complement the yarns, I have managed to achieve some wonderful results and now have bright, exciting bags to match every outfit.

Gauge

12 stitches and 14 rows to 4 in. over st st on US 15 needles using one strand each of A and B held together, although gauge is not crucial in felting.

Abbreviations

See page 125.

Bag

Using US 11 circular needle and one strand each of A and B held together, cast on 75 sts.

Join the cast on row into a circle, ensuring that the knitting is not twisted, and place a marker to establish the beginning of the round.

Round 1: [K1, p1] to last st, k1.

Round 2: [P1, k1] to last st, p1.

Rep rounds 1–2 twice more.

Round 7: [K14, inc] five times. (80 sts)

Change to US 15 circular needle and cont in knit stitch.

Knit 10 rounds.

Shape sides

Slip marker to the right-hand needle and start the shaping as folls:

Round 18: K4, M1, k32, M1, k8, M1, k32, M1, k4. (84 sts)

Knit 10 rounds.

Round 29: K5, M1, k32, M1, k10, M1, k32, M1, k5. (88 sts)

Knit 10 rounds.

Round 40: K6, M1, k32, M1, k12, M1, k32, M1, k6. (92 sts)

Knit 15 rounds.

Shape base

Slip marker to the right-hand needle and start the shaping as folls:

Round 56: K6, k2tog, k30, k2togtbl, k12, k2tog, k30, k2togtbl, k6. (88 sts)

Round 57: K5, k2tog, k30, k2togtbl, k10, k2tog, k30, k2togtbl, k5. (84 sts)

Round 58: K4, k2tog, k30, k2togtbl, k8, k2tog, k30, k2togtbl, k4. (80 sts)

Round 59: K3, k2tog, k30, k2togtbl, k6, k2tog, k30, k2togtbl, k3. (76 sts)

Round 60: K2, k2tog, k30, k2togtbl, k4, k2tog, k30, k2togtbl, k2. (72 sts)

Round 61: K1, k2tog, k30, k2togtbl, k2, k2tog, k30, k2togtbl, k1. (68 sts)

Round 62: K2tog, k30, k2togtbl, k2tog, k30, k2togtbl. (64 sts)

Join base

Turn the bag inside out and push 32 sts along to each needle point. Put both needle points together and, using another knitting needle (the same size as the circular needle or a size larger), knit tog the first st on each needle point. Knit tog the second stitch on each needle point, then slip the first st over the second st, so binding off (not too tightly) and joining the base of the bag at the same time. Rep until all sts are bound off.

Handle tabs (make four)

Using US 11 needles and one strand of A, cast on 4 sts.
  Knit 10 rows.
  Bind off.

Large flower

Using US 11 needles and one strand of wool or mohair, cast on 95 sts.
  Work flower in colored stripes for best effect.
Row 1: Knit.
Row 2: P1, p2tog, p1, p2togtbl, *p3, p2tog, p1, p2togtbl; rep from * to last st, p1.
(71 sts)
Row 3: *Skpo, k1, k2tog, k1; rep from * to last 5 sts, skpo, k1, k2tog. (47 sts)
Row 4: P3tog, *p1, p3tog; rep from * to the end of the row. (23 sts)
Row 5: Sk2po, *k1, sk2po; rep from * to the end of the row. (11 sts)
  Beginning with a purl row, work 2 rows st st.
  Leaving a 15 in. tail, cut yarn. Thread tail through rem sts and pull up tightly. Thread tail into knitter's sewing needle and join seam to complete flower.

Small flower

Using US 11 needles and one strand of wool or mohair, cast on 63 sts.
  Work flower in colored stripes for best effect.
Row 1: Knit.
Row 2: P1, p2tog, p1, p2togtbl, *p3, p2tog, p1, p2togtbl; rep from * to last st, p1.
(47 sts)
Row 3: *Skpo, k1, k2tog, k1; rep from * to last 5 sts, skpo, k1, k2tog. (31 sts)
Row 4: P3tog, *p1, p3tog; rep from * to the end of the row. (15 sts)
Row 5: Sk2po, *k1, sk2po; rep from * to the end of the row. (7 sts)
  Leaving a 15 in. tail, cut yarn. Thread tail through rem sts and pull up tightly. Thread tail into knitter's sewing needle and join seam to complete flower.

Leaf cluster

Using one strand of pure wool or mohair and US 10 knitting needles, cast on 15 sts.
Row 1: *Bind off 14 sts, slip rem st onto the left-hand needle, cast on 14 sts; *rep from * two or three more times. Leaving a 20 in. tail, cut yarn and fasten off.

The Noro Kureyon yarn knits up to give a striped effect, so for this bag I blended it with one strand of pure wool yarn to get a more subtle variegated effect.

To finish

Using tails of yarn and following the photograph for position, sew the leaves and flowers in a group to the front of the bag. You can sew a decorative bead into the center of each flower if you wish.

Measure the space between the slots in the bag handles and mark the positions with pins on the inside of the top of the bag. Thread the knitter's sewing needle or bodkin with one strand of A and sew one narrow end of a strip to each marked point, about ¼ in. down from the top edge. Thread the strips through the slots in the plastic handles. Sew the other narrow end of each strip to the inside of the bag, about ¼ in. below the first end.

Wrap the plastic handles tightly in bubble wrap and, with the bag right side out, fold the handles into the inside of the bag; this will protect them during the felting process in the washing machine. Close the bag opening with a safety pin or something similar to stop the handles from falling out.

If you want to use a wooden, beaded, or bamboo handle that cannot be put through the wash cycle, then sew one end of each strip in place as described. Felt the bag, then thread the felted strips through the slots and sew the free ends in place.

Darn in all loose ends.

Following the instructions on pages 123–124, machine-wash the bag to felt it.

You can sew on a large snap to fasten the bag if desired.

rust stripe bag

This bag is knitted following the pattern for the Variegated Stripe Bag, but using Knitting4fun Pure Wool in Rust for A and Noro Kureyon 201 for B. The flowers are worked in toning pure wools and leftover Noro Kureyon.

half bobble bag

You will need
- 5¼oz of Knitting4fun Natural Merino Pure Wool in Light Gray (A)
- 5¼oz of Knitting4fun Natural Merino Pure Wool in Dark Gray (B)
- US 11 (24 in. long) circular needle
- US 15 (24 in. or 32 in. long) circular needle
- Two US 15 double-pointed needles
- Knitter's sewing needle or bodkin for sewing
- Large snap (optional)

Finished size

Bag measures approx 10 in. high by 11½ in. wide.

My bobble addiction crept in again with this bag, but maybe I wasn't fully bobble crazy that day, as I made half the bag plain and only half with bobbles.

I chose these colors to go with a particular outfit, but this is a bag design that looks fantastic knitted in any two shades of one color, two toning colors, or, if you are feeling bold, in two clashing colors. Imagine it in chocolate brown and turquoise or in fuchsia pink and bright orange.

The handles for this bag are knitted i-cords, but to complement the bobble theme, the ends are tied in knots and pushed through the knitted bag fabric before felting. The knitting felts tightly around the base of the handles and the knots felt into chunky bobbles, which look great.

Gauge

12 stitches and 14 rows to 4 in. over st st on US 15 needles using two strands of A held together, although gauge is not crucial in felting.

Abbreviations

MB = make bobble: with two strands of contrast color (k1, p1, k1) into next st, turn p3, turn k3, turn p3, turn sk2po, slip the stitch back onto the left-hand needle and knit into it again using main color; cut contrast yarn, pull ends of contrast yarn tight to form the bobble, knot ends together, and sew them into the back of the bobble before felting. Alternatively, strand contrast color on the wrong side between bobbles and cut yarn at the end of each bobble row.

See also page 125.

Bag

Using US 11 circular needle and two strands of A held together, cast on 80 sts.

Join the cast on row into a circle, ensuring that the knitting is not twisted, and place a marker to establish the beginning of the round.

Round 1: [K1, p1] to the end of the row.

Round 2: [P1, k1] to the end of the row.

Rep rounds 1–2 once more then rep round 1 once more.

On the last row, mark the positions of the handles with four safety pins, placing them 10 sts, 30 sts, 50 sts, and 70 sts from the marker.

Round 6: [K19, inc] four times. (84 sts)

Change to US 15 circular needle and cont in knit stitch.

Knit 7 rounds.

Shape sides

Slip marker to the right-hand needle and start the shaping as folls:

Round 14: K4, M1, k34, M1, k8, M1, k34, M1, k4. (88 sts)

Knit 7 rounds.

Round 22: K5, M1, k34, M1, k10, M1, k34, M1, k5. (92 sts)

Knit 3 rounds.

Break A and join in 2 strands of B.

Knit 2 rounds.

Round 27: K6, M1, k34, M1, k12, M1, k34, M1, k6. (96 sts)

Round 28 (bobble round): [K7, MB] to the end of the row.

Knit 6 rounds.

Round 34 (bobble round): K4 [MB, k7] to last 4 sts, MB, k3.

Knit 6 rounds.

Round 41 (bobble round): As round 28.

Knit 6 rounds.

Round 48 (bobble round): As round 34.

Knit 6 rounds.

Round 55 (bobble round): As round 28.

Knit 5 rounds.

Shape base

Slip marker to the right-hand needle and start the shaping as folls:

Round 61: K5, k2tog, k34, k2togtbl, k10, k2tog, k34, k2togtbl, k5. (92 sts)

Round 62: K4, k2tog, k34, k2togtbl, k8, k2tog, k34, k2togtbl, k4. (88 sts)

Round 63: K3, k2tog, k34, k2togtbl, k6, k2tog, k34, k2togtbl, k3. (84 sts)
Round 64: K2, k2tog, k34, k2togtbl, k4, k2tog, k34, k2togtbl, k2. (80 sts)
Round 65: K1, k2tog, k34, k2togtbl, k2, k2tog, k34, k2togtbl, k1. (76 sts)
Round 66: K2tog, k34, k2togtbl, k2tog, k34, k2togtbl. (72 sts)

Join base

Turn the bag inside out and push 36 sts along to each needle point. Put both needle points together and, using another knitting needle (the same size as the circular needle or a size larger), knit tog the first st on each needle point. Knit tog the second stitch on each needle point, then slip the first st over the second st, so binding off (not too tightly) and joining the base of the bag at the same time. Rep until all sts are bound off.

Handles (make two)

Using US 15 double-pointed needles and two strands of B held together, cast on 4 sts.

Knit 1 row.

Switch needles in your hands, so the needle with the stitches on is in your left hand again. Slide the stitches to the other end of the needle and, pulling the yarn across the back of the stitches, knit the row again. The first three or four rows will be flat but don't worry, after that the knitting will become tubular. Before knitting the first stitch of each row, give the yarn a tug to make the strand across the back disappear.

Cont in this way, sliding and knitting, until the handle is the required length. As the handles will shrink by approximately one-third during felting, I usually knit about 50–60 rows for a short hand-held handle, 100 rows for a longer hand-held handle, and 120–140 rows for a shoulder handle.

Bind off.

To finish

Thread the ends of the handles through the knitting at the point marked by the safety pins, about 5 rows down from the top edge. Tie the ends in a tight knot on the right side. Using the knitter's sewing needle and one strand of D, sew through the knots, sewing them to the knitting so that they don't move during the felting process.

Darn in all loose ends.

Following the instructions on pages 123–124, machine-wash the bag to felt it.

You can sew on a large snap to fasten the bag if desired.

My bobble addiction crept in again with this bag, but maybe I wasn't fully bobble crazy that day, as I made half the bag plain and only half with bobbles.

violets are blue

You will need

- 8¾oz of Knitting4fun Pure Wool in Black (A)
- Small amounts of Knitting4fun Pure Wool in Purple, Damson, and Apple Green
- Small amount of Knitting4fun Space-dyed Pure Wool in Purple
- Small amounts of Knitting4fun Fine Pure Wool in Lavender and Yellow
- US 11 (16 in. or 24 in. long) circular needle
- US 15 (24 in. or 32 in. long) circular needle
- Pair of US 10 knitting needles
- Pair of US 11 knitting needles
- Pair of plastic bag handles
- Knitter's sewing needle or bodkin for sewing
- Large snap (optional)
- Decorative beads (optional)

Finished size

Bag measures approx 9 in. high by 11½ in. wide.

This bag was inspired by the most perfect little black evening dress that I saw in a boutique. I wanted to make a black bag to go with it and knitted a variety of flowers in different shades of lavender, purple, and violet to embellish it.

Some of the flowers are sewn straight onto the bag, but a couple of the larger ones are sewn onto brooch backs. This means that I can wear them as a corsage on the dress to match it beautifully with the bag.

This has been one of the most popular of my bags and I have knitted several versions with different-colored flowers. On the Roses Are Red bag (see page 100) I used black crystal beads to decorate the centers of the flowers and add a bit of bling!

Choose yarn colors that match or complement your outfit to make your own version of this bag and decorate the flowers with beads or simple embroidery stitches, whichever you prefer.

Gauge

12 stitches and 14 rows to
4 in. over st st on US 15
needles using two strands of
A held together, although
gauge is not crucial in felting.

Abbreviations

See page 125.

Bag

Using US 11 circular needle and two strands of A held together, cast on 80 sts.

Join the cast on row into a circle, ensuring that the knitting is not twisted, and place a marker to establish the beginning of the round.

Round 1: [K1, p1] to the end of the row.

Round 2: [P1, k1] to the end of the row.

Rep rounds 1–2 twice more.

Round 7: [K19, inc] four times. (84 sts)

Change to US 15 circular needle and cont in knit stitch.

Knit 10 rounds.

Shape sides

Slip marker to the right-hand needle and start the shaping as folls:

Round 18: K4, M1, k34, M1, k8, M1, k34, M1, k4. (88 sts)

Knit 10 rounds.

Round 29: K5, M1, k34, M1, k10, M1, k34, M1, k5. (92 sts)

Knit 10 rounds.

Round 39: K6, M1, k34, M1, k12, M1, k34, M1, k6. (96 sts)

Knit 15 rounds.

Shape base

Slip marker to the right-hand needle and start the shaping as folls:

Round 55: K6, k2tog, k32, k2togtbl, k12, k2tog, k32, k2togtbl, k6. (92 sts)

Round 56: K5, k2tog, k32, k2togtbl, k10, k2tog, k32, k2togtbl, k5. (88 sts)

Round 57: K4, k2tog, k32, k2togtbl, k8, k2tog, k32, k2togtbl, k4. (84 sts)

Round 58: K3, k2tog, k32, k2togtbl, k6, k2tog, k32, k2togtbl, k3. (80 sts)

Round 59: K2, k2tog, k32, k2togtbl, k4, k2tog, k32, k2togtbl, k2. (76 sts)

Round 60: K1, k2tog, k32, k2togtbl, k2, k2tog, k32, k2togtbl, k1. (72 sts)

Round 61: K2tog, k32, k2togtbl, k2tog, k32, k2togtbl. (68 sts)

Join base

Turn the bag inside out and push 34 sts along to each needle point. Put both needle points together and, using another knitting needle (the same size as the circular needle or a size larger), knit tog the first st on each needle point. Knit tog the second stitch on each needle point, then slip the first st over the second st, so binding off (not too tightly) and joining the base of the bag at the same time. Rep until all sts are bound off.

Handle tabs (make four)
Using US 11 needles and one strand of A, cast on 4 sts.
  Knit 8 rows.
  Bind off.

Large flower
Using one strand of pure wool and US 10 knitting needles, cast on 11 sts.
Row 1: Knit 10 sts, turn.
Row 2: Sl1, k8, turn.
Row 3: Sl1, k7, turn.
Row 4: Sl1, k6, turn.
Row 5: Sl1, k5, turn.
Row 6: Sl1, k4, turn.
Row 7: Sl1, k3, turn.
Row 8: Sl1, knit to the end of the row.
Row 9: Sl1, k1 psso, then bind off all sts.
Leave rem st on needle and cast on 10 more sts. (11 sts)
  Rep rows 1–9 four or five times more to give five or six petals, as desired.
  Leaving a 20 in. tail, cut yarn. Thread knitter's sewing needle or bodkin with tail and sew through the edge of each petal and gather up, pulling the petals into a ring. Sew through the center to hold the flower together.

Small flower
Using one strand of pure wool and US 10 knitting needles, cast on 9 sts.
Row 1: Knit 8 sts, turn.
Row 2: Sl1, k6, turn.
Row 3: Sl1, k5, turn.
Row 4: Sl1, k4, turn.
Row 5: Sl1, k3, turn.
Row 6: Sl1, knit to the end of the row.
Row 7: Sl1, k1 psso, then bind off all sts.
  Leave rem st on needle and cast on 8 more sts. (9 sts)
  Rep rows 1–7 four or five more times to give five or six petals, as desired.
  Finish as for Large Flower.

This bag was inspired by the most perfect little black evening dress that I saw in a boutique.

Daisy

Using one strand of pure wool and US 10 knitting needles, cast on 7 sts.

Row 1: *Bind off 6 sts, slip rem st onto the left-hand needle, cast on 6 sts; *rep from * five or six more times. Leaving a 20 in. tail, cut yarn. Thread knitter's sewing needle or bodkin with tail and sew through the edge of each petal and gather up, pulling the petals into a ring. Sew through the center to hold the flower together.

Leaf cluster

Using one strand of pure wool and US 10 knitting needles, cast on 15 sts.

Row 1: *Bind off 14 sts, slip rem st onto the left-hand needle, cast on 14 sts; *rep from * two or three more times. Leaving a 20 in. tail, cut yarn and fasten off.

To finish

Using tails of yarn and following the photograph for position, sew the flowers and leaves in a group to the front of the bag. You can embroider the center of each flower with a French knot or sew on a decorative bead.

Measure the space between the slots in the bag handles and mark the positions with pins on the inside of the top of the bag. Thread the knitter's sewing needle or bodkin with one strand of A and sew one narrow end of a strip to each marked point, about ¼ in. down from the top edge. Thread the strips through the slots in the plastic handles. Sew the other narrow end of each strip to the inside of the bag, about ¼ in. below the first end.

Wrap the plastic handles tightly in bubble wrap and, with the bag right side out, fold the handles into the inside of the bag; this will protect them during the felting process in the washing machine. Close the bag opening with a safety pin or something similar to stop the handles from falling out.

If you want to use a wooden, beaded, or bamboo handle that cannot be put through the wash cycle, then sew one end of each strip in place as described. Felt the bag, then thread the felted strips through the slots and sew the free ends in place.

Darn in all loose ends.

Following the instructions on pages 123–124, machine-wash the bag to felt it.

You can sew on a large snap to fasten the bag if desired.

roses are red

Made in exactly the same way as Violets Are Blue, this bag rings the changes by using red instead of blue yarns for the flowers.

small floral bag

You will need

- 5¼oz of Knitting4fun Pure Wool in Apple Green (A)
- 3½oz of Ice Catena in color 6513 (B)
- Small amounts of Knitting4fun Pure Wool in Purple, Orange, and Yellow
- US 11 (16 in. or 24 in. long) circular needle
- US 13 (24 in. long) circular needle
- Pair of US 13 double-pointed needles
- Pair of US 8 knitting needles
- Knitter's sewing needle or bodkin for sewing
- Large snap (optional)

Finished size

Bag measures approx 9 in. high by 8 in. wide.

After a long winter, spring came at last and the early pansies, beautiful bulbs, and primroses were all blooming in my garden. This bag was inspired by those lovely spring colors.

The bag is knitted in apple green pure wool and knitted with it is an acrylic yarn that has lots of fresh colors running through it. It is a slightly textured yarn and when felted, gives a bouclé effect.

The bag is a dainty size and is very quick and easy to make, ideal for a party. I've been known to knit one the day before I'm going out and to arrive at the party with a bag that is still just a tiny bit damp from the felting process.

The flowers, which are also very easy to make, are knitted using pure wool in a variety of colors. They are stitched in place and can be embellished by sewing a French knot or a bead into the center. You can make as many or as few flowers as you wish and arrange them in groups or scatter them individually around the bag.

Gauge

14 stitches and 16 rows to 4 in. over st st on US 13 needles using one strand each of A and B held together, although gauge is not crucial in felting.

Abbreviations

See page 125.

Bag

Using US 11 circular needle and one strand each of A and B held together, cast on 55 sts.

Join the cast on row into a circle, ensuring that the knitting is not twisted, and place a marker to establish the beginning of the round.

Round 1: [K1, p1] to last st, k1.

Round 2: [P1, k1] to last st, p1.

Rep rounds 1–2 once more, then rep round 1 once more.

Round 6: [K10, inc] five times. (60 sts)

Change to US 13 circular needle and cont in knit stitch.

Knit 10 rounds.

Shape sides

Slip marker to the right-hand needle and start the shaping as folls:

Round 17: K3, M1, k24, M1, k6, M1, k24, M1, k3. (64 sts)

Knit 12 rounds.

Round 30: K4, M1, k24, M1, k8, M1, k24, M1, k4. (68 sts)

Knit 14 rounds.

Shape base

Slip marker to the right-hand needle and start the shaping as folls:

Round 58: K4, k2tog, k22, k2togtbl, k8, k2tog, k22, k2togtbl, k4. (64 sts)

Round 59: K3, k2tog, k22, k2togtbl, k6, k2tog, k22, k2togtbl, k3. (70 sts)

Round 60: K2, k2tog, k22, k2togtbl, k4, k2tog, k22, k2togtbl, k2. (56 sts)

Round 61: K1, k2tog, k22, k2togtbl, k2, k2tog, k22, k2togtbl, k1. (52 sts)

Round 62: K2tog, k22, k2togtbl, k2tog, k22, k2togtbl. (48 sts)

Join base

Turn the bag inside out and push 24 sts along to each needle point. Put both needle points together and, using another knitting needle (the same size as the circular needle or a size larger), knit tog the first st on each needle point. Knit tog the second stitch on each needle point, then slip the first st over the second st, so binding off (not too tightly) and joining the base of the bag at the same time. Rep until all sts are bound off.

Handles (make two)

Using US 15 double-pointed needles and two strands of A held together, cast on 4 sts.

Knit 1 row.

Switch needles in your hands, so the needle with the stitches on is in your left hand again. Slide the stitches to the other end of the needle and, pulling the yarn across the back of the stitches, knit the row again. The first three or four rows will be flat but don't worry, after that the knitting will become tubular. Before knitting the first stitch of each row, give the yarn a tug to make the strand across the back disappear.

Cont in this way, sliding and knitting, until the handle is the required length. As the handles will shrink by approximately one-third during felting, I usually knit about 50–60 rows for a short hand-held handle, 100 rows for a longer hand-held handle, and 120–140 rows for a shoulder handle.

Bind off.

Flower

Using one strand of pure wool and US 8 knitting needles, cast on 7 sts.

Row 1: *Bind off 6 sts, slip rem st onto the left-hand needle, cast on 6 sts; *rep from * five or six more times. Leaving a 20 in. tail, cut yarn. Thread knitter's sewing needle or bodkin with tail and sew through the edge of each petal and gather up, pulling the petals into a ring. Sew through the center to hold the flower together.

To finish

Using tails of yarn and following the photograph for position, sew the flowers to the front of the bag. You can sew a decorative bead or embroider a French knot into the center of each flower.

Using the knitter's sewing needle and A, sew the free end of the handle to the opposite top edge of the bag.

Darn in all loose ends.

Following the instructions on pages 123–124, machine-wash the bag to felt it.

You can sew on a large snap to fasten the bag if desired.

After a long winter, spring came at last and the early pansies, beautiful bulbs, and primroses were all blooming in my garden.

pom-pom perfect

You will need

- 7oz of Knitting4fun Pure Wool in Fuchsia (A)
- 5oz of Knitting4fun Pure Wool in Lavender (B)
- ¾oz of Crystal Palace Yarns Popcorn in Violet Plums 442 (C)
- ¾oz of Knitting4fun Pure Wool in Purple (D)
- US 11 (24 in. long) circular needle
- US 15 (24 in. or 32 in. long) circular needle
- Two US 15 double-pointed needles
- Pair of US 11 knitting needles
- Button or toggle for fastening
- Knitter's sewing needle or bodkin for sewing

Finished size

Bag measures approx 10 in. high by 12 in. wide.

I found this amazing popcorn yarn and just had to have a ball of it—in the same way as I had to have the hundreds of other yarns that I have stashed away around the house.

Having made the gray Half Bobble Bag (see page 92), I liked the idea of half the bag in one color and the other half in another color. Using the popcorn yarn in a textured band around the middle divided and balanced the plain colors and was the perfect way to use up my one ball.

The knotted handles and the tab for the button closure are knitted in a third color, picked out from the popcorn yarn.

This design lends itself to being made in many different colorways, as there are so many pom-pom and popcorn yarns in such wonderful color combinations. Alternatively, the popcorn yarn could be added in rows randomly as you knit the bag, with just one main color of pure wool used throughout.

Gauge

12 stitches and 14 rows to 4 in. over st st on US 15 needles using two strands of A held together, although gauge is not crucial in felting.

Abbreviations

See page 125.

Bag

Using US 11 circular needle and two strands of A held together, cast on 80 sts.

Join the cast on row into a circle, ensuring that the knitting is not twisted, and place a marker to establish the beginning of the round.

Round 1: [K1, p1] to the end of the row.

Round 2: [P1, k1] to the end of the row.

Rep rounds 1–2 once more, then rep round 1 once more.

On the last row, mark the positions of the handles with four safety pins, placing them 10 sts, 30 sts, 50 sts, and 70 sts from the marker.

Round 6: [K19, inc] four times. (84 sts)

Change to US 15 circular needle and cont in knit stitch.

Knit 12 rounds.

Shape sides

Slip marker to the right-hand needle and start the shaping as folls:

Round 19: K4, M1, k34, M1, k8, M1, k34, M1, k4. (88 sts)

Knit 6 rounds.

Cut A and join in 1 strand each of B and C.

Purl 6 rounds. Purling the stitches helps to keep the textured yarn on the right side of the knitting.

Cut C and join in a second strand of B.

Round 32: K5, M1, k34, M1, k10, M1, k34, M1, k5. (92 sts)

Knit 12 rounds.

Round 45: K6, M1, k34, M1, k12, M1, k34, M1, k6. (96 sts)

Knit 17 rounds.

Shape base

Slip marker to the right-hand needle and start the shaping as folls:

Round 63: K6, k2tog, k32, k2togtbl, k12, k2tog, k32, k2togtbl, k6. (92 sts)

Round 64: K5, k2tog, k32, k2togtbl, k10, k2tog, k32, k2togtbl, k5. (88 sts)

Round 65: K4, k2tog, k32, k2togtbl, k8, k2tog, k32, k2togtbl, k4. (84 sts)

Round 66: K3, k2tog, k32, k2togtbl, k6, k2tog, k32, k2togtbl, k3. (80 sts)

Round 67: K2, k2tog, k32, k2togtbl, k4, k2tog, k32, k2togtbl, k2. (76 sts)

Round 68: K1, k2tog, k32, k2togtbl, k2, k2tog, k32, k2togtbl, k1. (72 sts)

Round 69: K2tog, k32, k2togtbl, k2tog, k32, k2togtbl. (68 sts)

Join base

Turn the bag inside out and push 34 sts along to each needle point. Put both needle points together and, using another knitting needle (the same size as the circular needle or a size larger), knit tog the first st on each needle point. Knit tog the second stitch on each needle point, then slip the first st over the second st, so binding off (not too tightly) and joining the base of the bag at the same time. Rep until all sts are bound off.

Flap

Using US 11 knitting needles and one strand of D, pick up 14 sts evenly along one top edge between safety pins.

Knit 16 rows.

Row 17: K2togtbl, k10, k2tog. (12 sts)

Row 18: K4, bind off 4 sts, knit to the end of the row. (8 sts)

Row 19: K2togtbl, k2, cast on 3 sts, k2, k2tog. (9 sts)

Row 20: Knit.

Row 21: K2togtbl, k5, k2tog. (7 sts)

Bind off.

Handles (make two)

Using US 15 double-pointed needles and two strands of D held together, cast on 4 sts.

Knit 1 row.

Switch needles in your hands, so the needle with the stitches on is in your left hand again. Slide the stitches to the other end of the needle and, pulling the yarn across the back of the stitches, knit the row again. The first three or four rows will be flat but don't worry, after that the knitting will become tubular. Before knitting the first stitch of each row, give the yarn a tug to make the strand across the back disappear.

Cont in this way, sliding and knitting, until the handle is the required length. As the handles will shrink by approximately one-third during felting, I usually knit about 50–60 rows for a short hand-held handle, 100 rows for a longer hand-held handle, and 120–140 rows for a shoulder handle.

Bind off.

To finish

Thread the ends of the handles through the knitting at the point marked by the safety pins, about 5 rows down from the top edge. Tie the ends in a tight knot on the right side. Using the knitter's sewing needle and one strand of D, sew through the knots, sewing them to the knitting so that they don't move during the felting process.

Darn in all loose ends.

Following the instructions on pages 123–124, machine-wash the bag to felt it.

You can sew on a large snap to fasten the bag if desired.

I found this amazing popcorn yarn and just had to have a ball of it—in the same way as I had to have the hundreds of other yarns that I have stashed away around the house.

yarns and techniques

The basic bag shapes are very easy to knit, so novice knitters can approach the projects with confidence. The felting process is equally simple, as the washing machine does all the hard work for you. You'll also find in this chapter all the information you need on choosing yarns for your bags.

choosing and using yarns

I knitted the bags in this book in a variety of yarns and each pattern tells you what I used to make the bag shown: turn to page 126 for suppliers. However, one of the wonderful things about felting is that you can experiment with yarns, so I have given ideas for substitutes if you want to try something different.

Yarns used

Here are specifications for all the yarns used in the bag patterns. The number in brackets following the yardage is the Standard Yarn Weight System number. For substitute yarns, turn to pages 113–118.

- Knitting4fun Pure Wool, 100% pure wool, 3½oz/218yd (4)
- Knitting4fun Chunky Pure Wool, 100% pure wool, 3½oz/110yd (5)
- Knitting4fun Space-dyed Pure Wool, 100% pure wool, 3½oz/164yd (4)
- Knitting4fun Natural Merino Wool, 100% pure wool, 3½oz/218yd (4)
- Knitting4fun Fine Pure Wool, 100% pure wool, 3½oz/273yd (3)
- Knitting4fun Banana Fiber Kaleidoscope Yarn, 100% banana fiber, 7oz/140–164yd (5)
- Knitting4fun Recycled Sari Silk Yarn, 100% silk, 7oz/140–164yd (5)
- Colinette Giotto, 50% cotton, 40% rayon, 10% nylon, 3½oz/157yd (4)

- Crystal Palace Yarns Popcorn, 100% nylon, 1¾oz/81yd (5)
- Elle Pizzazz, 65% acrylic, 35% polyester, 1¾oz/60yd (5)
- Filati FF Park, 68% polyester, 32% nylon, 1¾oz/44yd (5)
- Ice Long Eyelash, 100% polyester, 1¾oz/38yd (5)
- Ice Catena, 100% polyamide, 1¾oz/110yd (5)
- Katia Cancan, 100% polyester, 1¾oz/46yd (5)
- Lang Mille Colori, 50% new wool, 50% acrylic, 1¾oz/100yd (4)
- Noro Kureyon, 100% pure wool, 1¾oz/110yd (4)

Substituting yarns

I have used my own Knitting4fun pure wool yarns throughout this book as, having tried and tested them many times, I know that they felt beautifully at 40 degrees in the washing machine, and that they keep their color. However, if you want to use a different yarn to a specified project yarn, here are some suggestions. I can't guarantee the results, but I have used these yarns to make felted projects.

Each bag knitting pattern will give the quantity of the yarn I have specified that is needed to knit it. However, you can't just buy the same quantity of the substitute yarn, as balls of different brands of yarn, even of the same type and ball weight, can contain different yardages of yarn. Check the yardage per ball of the specified pattern yarn (see the listing opposite) and multiply that figure by the quantity needed to establish the total yardage needed for the project, then buy the same yardage of the substitute yarn.

It is always a good idea to knit and felt a large swatch of a substitute yarn before knitting up a whole project (see Felting the Knitting, page 123). Keep notes on how the yarn felts and when you are happy with the result, go ahead and knit your project.

The substitute yarns

As a substitute for any of the Knitting4fun yarns you can try:

- Brown Sheep Company Inc, Top of the Lamb Worsted, 100% wool, 1 skein/190yd
- Brown Sheep Company Inc, Lamb's Pride Worsted 85% wool, 15% mohair, 1 skein/190yd
- Cascade Yarns, Cascade 220 Wool, 100% Peruvian wool, 3½oz/220yd

Pure purple

Plant pot

Flower power

Paint box bag

Listed here are suggestions for substitutes for the fancy yarns used to make the bags. For substitutes for the Knitting4fun yarns, turn to page 113. There is such a huge range of yarns available that generally I have specified types rather than brands, so you are sure to find something suitable in your yarn store.

PURE PURPLE, PAGE 10
Yarn used
- Knitting4fun Pure Wool in Purple and Damson, 100% pure wool, 3½oz/218yd
- Elle Pizzazz in Poison 252, 65% acrylic, 35% polyester, 1⅞oz /60yd

I used two toning shades of Knitting4fun Pure Wool to make a variegated color to match the colors in the Elle Pizzazz yarn.
Substitute yarn
Any eyelash yarn will work for the top edge, but the textures may be different.

PLANT POT, PAGE 14
Yarn used
- Knitting4fun Pure Wool in Rust, 100% pure wool, 3½oz/218yd
- Colinette Giotto in Windfall 149, 50% cotton, 40% rayon, 10% nylon, 3½oz/157yd
- Knitting4fun Pure Wool in Apple Green, Yellow, and Cream, 100% pure wool, 3½oz /218yd

Colinette Giotto gives texture and sheen once the bag is felted.
Substitute yarn
Any ribbon yarn will give a similar, though not identical, effect.

FLOWER POWER, PAGE 18
Yarn used
- Knitting4fun Pure Wool in Lime Green and Turquoise, 100% pure wool, 3½oz/218yd
- Colinette Giotto in Lagoon 138, 50% cotton, 40% rayon, 10% nylon, 3½oz /157yd

The mix of colors and yarns gives a tweedy look.
Substitute yarn
Any ribbon yarn will give a similar effect, as long as you choose the color carefully.

PAINT BOX BAG, PAGE 22
Yarn used
- Knitting4fun Pure Wool, 100% pure wool, 3½oz/218yd

It's the mix of vibrant colors make this bag so striking.
Substitute yarn
Choose a good range of strong colors in a substitute for Knitting4fun yarn.

JAZZY BAG, PAGE 30
Yarn used
- Knitting4fun Pure Wool in Turquoise, 100% pure wool, 3½oz/218yd
- Elle Pizzazz in Carnival 253, 65% acrylic, 35% polyester, 1⅞oz /60yd
- Ice Long Eyelash in Fuchsia, 100% polyester, 1¾oz /38yd

I love the heavily textured, dreadlock-type fronds of the Elle Pizzazz yarn.
Substitute yarn
Any mix of eyelash yarns will create a fluffy top edge.

Jazzy book bag

Jazzy bag

JAZZY BOOK BAG, PAGE 34

Yarn used

- Knitting4fun Pure Wool in Turquoise, 100% pure wool, 3½oz/218yd
- Filati FF Park in color 45, 68% polyester, 32% nylon, 1¾oz /44yd
- Ice Catena in Aqua/Green/Blue, 100% polyamide, 1¾oz /110yd

The pom-pom yarn makes a thick, spongy fabric to help protect a laptop.

Substitute yarn

Use any eyelash, pom-pom, or popcorn yarns for this bag.

ORANGE FLUFF AND BOBBLE, PAGE 36

Yarn used

- Knitting4fun Natural Merino Wool in Gray, 100% pure wool, 3½oz /218yd
- Ice Long Eyelash in Orange 8814, 100% polyester, 1¾oz /38yd
- Knitting4fun Pure Wool in Orange, 100% pure wool, 3½oz/218yd

The Ice Long Eyelash yarn gives a thick, luxurious trim to the top of the bag.

Substitute yarn

Any eyelash yarn will work: the longer and thicker it is, the better the effect.

ANYTHING GOES STASH BAG, PAGE 40

Yarn used

- Knitting4fun Pure Wool, 100% pure wool, 3½oz/218yd
- Any eyelash, feather, or ribbon yarns

This is a stash-busting bag design.

Substitute yarn

Any leftover eyelash, feather, ribbon, or other textured yarns.

RETRO BUTTON BAG, PAGE 46

Yarn used

- Knitting4fun Pure Wool in Brown, 100% pure wool, 3½oz/218yd
- Katia Cancan in Brown, 100% polyester, 1¾oz /46yd

The Katia Cancan yarn has a long double eyelash and gives a very fluffy top edge.

Substitute yarn

Any long eyelash yarn will work well.

SLIP STITCH HONEYCOMB, PAGE 50

Yarn used

- Knitting4fun Pure Wool in Fuchsia and Orange, 100% pure wool, 3½oz/218yd
- Ice Long Eyelash in Fuchsia and Orange, 100% polyester, 1¾oz /38yd

Knitting alternate rows of each color of Ice Long Eyelash gives a variegated trim.

Substitute yarn

Any two colors of eyelash yarn will work for the fluffy top edge.

Orange fluff and bobble

Anything goes stash bag

Retro button bag

Slip stitch honeycomb

Red wool and ribbon

Cherry ripe

Recycled sari silk bag
Banana fiber bag

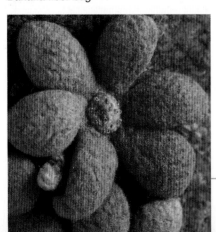

RED WOOL AND RIBBON, PAGE 56

Yarn used

- Knitting4fun Pure Wool in Red, 100% pure wool, 3½oz/218yd
- Colinette Giotto in Fire 71, 50% cotton, 40% rayon, 10% nylon, 3½oz /157yd

This bag makes good use of the tweedy effect the Colinette yarn produces when felted with a pure wool yarn.

Substitute yarn

You can use any ribbon yarn to create a similar effect.

CHERRY RIPE, PAGE 60

Yarn used

- Knitting4fun Natural Merino Wool in Dark Gray and Light Gray, 100% pure wool, 3½oz /218yd
- Knitting4fun Space-dyed Pure Wool in Red and Green, 100% pure wool, 3½oz /164yd

The space-dyed wool gives very subtle color changes to the cherries and leaves, making them look more realistic.

Substitute yarn

You can try using either Crystal Palace Yarns Fjord Print Worsted Wool or South West Trading, Karaoke Multi Wool Blend.

RECYCLED SARI SILK BAG, PAGE 66

Yarn used

- Knitting4fun Pure Wool in Fuchsia, 100% pure wool, 3½oz/218yd
- Knitting4fun Recycled Sari Silk Yarn, 100% silk, 7oz/140–164yd

The lovely bright colors in the Knitting4fun wool yarns match the bright colors in the recycled sari silk yarn.

Substitute yarn

You can use any recycled sari silk yarn for a similar effect.

BANANA FIBER BAG, PAGE 70

Yarn used

- Knitting4fun Pure Wool in Violet, 100% pure wool, 3½oz/218yd
- Knitting4fun Banana Fiber Kaleidoscope Yarn, 100% banana fiber, 7oz/140–164yd

The banana fiber yarn is another that works well with the colors of the Knitting4fun wool yarns.

Substitute yarn

You can use any banana fiber yarn for a similar effect.

Little saddle bag

LITTLE SADDLE BAG, PAGE 72

Yarn used

- Knitting4fun Pure Wool in Deep Pink, 100% pure wool, 3½oz/218yd
- Lang Mille Colori in color 65, 50% new wool, 50% acrylic, 1¾oz /100yd

The pure wool yarn traps the Mille Colori yarn and gives a slightly bouclé effect once felted.

Substitute yarn

You can try using either Crystal Palace Yarns Fjord Print Worsted Wool or South West Trading, Karaoke Multi Wool Blend.

ACORN AND OAK LEAF, PAGE 76

Yarn used

- Knitting4fun Pure Wool in Apple Green, Gold and Brown 100% pure wool, 3½oz/218yd
- Knitting4fun Space-dyed Pure Wool in Green, 100% pure wool, 3½oz /164yd
- Noro Kureyon in color 201, 100% pure wool, 1¾oz /110yd

Mixing the Kureyon with the plain-color wool yarn gives a more subtle effect to the striping of the Noro yarn and gives a firmer felt than if the Noro Kureyon is used alone.

Substitute yarn

You can try using any pure wool variegated yarn with a plain-colored pure wool yarn.

MONOCHROME JAZZ, PAGE 82

Yarn used

- Knitting4fun Pure Wool in black, 100% pure wool, 3½oz/218yd
- Elle Pizzazz in Zest 250, 65% acrylic, 35% polyester, 1¾oz /60yd
- Ice Long Eyelash in Black 7711, 100% polyester, 1¾oz /38yd

The mix of the Pizzazz yarn and Long Eyelash yarn create a really textural trim around the top of the bag.

Substitute yarn

You can mix any two types of eyelash yarn to create a similar, though not identical, effect.

VARIEGATED STRIPE BAG, PAGE 86

Yarn used

- Knitting4fun Pure Wool in Jade, 100% pure wool, 3½oz/218yd
- Noro Kureyon in color 173, 100% pure wool, 1¾oz /110yd

You can alter the look of a variegated yarn by knitting it together with a plain color that picks up some of the tones in the multi-colored yarn.

Substitute yarn

You can try using any pure wool variegated yarn with a plain-colored pure wool yarn.

Acorn and oak leaf

Monochrome jazz bag

Variegated stripe bag

Half bobble bag

Violets are blue

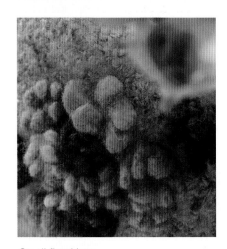

Small floral bag

HALF BOBBLE BAG, PAGE 92

Yarn used

- Knitting4fun Natural Merino Wool in Light Gray and Dark Gray, 100% pure wool, 3½oz /218yd

Mixing two shades of gray creates this understated yet sophisticated look.

Substitute yarn

Choose two shades of one color in a pure wool yarn to get this effect.

VIOLETS ARE BLUE, PAGE 96

Yarn used

- Knitting4fun Pure Wool in Black, Purple, Damson, and Apple Green, 100% pure wool, 3½oz/218yd
- Knitting4fun Space-dyed Pure Wool in Purple, 100% pure wool, 3½oz /164yd
- Knitting4fun Fine Pure Wool in Lavender and Yellow, 100% pure wool, 3½oz/273yd

The space-dyed yarn gives the flowers subtle color variations that make the most of the simple shapes.

Substitute yarn

You can try using either Crystal Palace Yarns Fjord Print Worsted Wool or South West Trading, Karaoke Multi Wool Blend.

SMALL FLORAL BAG, PAGE 102

Yarn used

- Knitting4fun Pure Wool in Apple Green, Purple, Orange, and Yellow, 100% pure wool, 3½oz/218yd
- Ice Catena in color 6513, 100% polyamide, 1¾oz /110yd

The Ice Catena is a ladder-type yarn so when it is combined with pure wool and felted, the wool traps the acrylic yarn and creates a bouclé effect on the surface.

Substitute yarn

You could use any ladder-type yarn mixed with a pure wool yarn to get a similar effect.

POM-POM PERFECT, PAGE 106

Yarn used

- Knitting4fun Pure Wool in Fuchsia, Purple and Lavender, 100% pure wool, 3½oz/218yd
- Crystal Palace Yarns Popcorn in Violet Plums 442, 100% nylon, 1¾oz/81yd

I love the texture and colors of the Popcorn yarn and they were easy to match with colors from the Knitting4fun range.

Substitute yarn

You can use any pom-pom or popcorn yarn for this bag.

Pom-pom perfect

handles, beads, and buttons

Quite a few of my knitted and felted bags have plastic handles and I have used both beads and buttons as embellishments. Suppliers for all of these items can be found on page 126.

I have used several different styles of handbag handles. They are made from durable plastic and come in a range of colors, shapes, and sizes.

You can find handles in some quite unusual colors and patterns that will complement the yarn colors you choose.

The buttons I have used are from various sources. Some are buttons that I have collected over the years, others are ones that I sell through my website. There is a huge range of buttons available through the Internet and the ones you choose will make your bags unique.

It is lovely to use up some of your own button stash, buttons that have memories attached to them, rather than leaving them hidden away out of sight in a box.

The beads that I have used to embellish the flowers on some of the bags are size 11 and size 15 seed beads and Czech and Swarovski crystals in various sizes.

knitting the bags

The patterns in this book are not complicated, so even if you are a beginner knitter you should be able to knit yourself a bag. In fact, the felting process hides a multitude of sins—uneven gauge, twisted stitches, and even dropped stitches disappear—so beginners have very little to worry about.

Knitting with a circular needle

The bags in this book are all knitted on a circular needle. I love using this type of needle as I don't have to sew up seams to finish the bag. There are circular needles available in plastic, bamboo, wood, metal, or resin, and it is really a matter of deciding which material you prefer to work with.

Some people seem to find using a circular needle difficult, but it is very easy provided the cord joining the two needle points is the correct length. If the cord is too short the stitches will be crammed together and will take every opportunity to jump off the needle tips. If the cord is too long, the stitches won't reach around from one needle point to the other. Each bag pattern tells you how long the cord needs to be, so make sure you get the right length when you buy your needle.

Once you have cast on the required number of stitches for the bag, they have to be spread evenly around the needle cord. When joining the stitches to knit the first round, you need to make sure that the row of cast on stitches is not twisted or the knitting will be twisted. This will mean having to start the project again.

Knit the first stitch quite tightly when joining the start and end of the cast on row. I wrap the tail from the cast on around the yarn I am about to work with so that it tightens up the first stitch and joins the ends securely.

Remember to slip a round marker onto the needle between the first and last stitches so that you can easily see where the beginning of the round is. This is necessary so that you can tell when you have knitted the required number of rounds, and to keep track of your position when you are decreasing.

You can buy plastic, metal, and beaded round markers, but a loop of contrast-colored yarn will work just as well. However, if you do use a yarn round marker, be careful not to knit it as though it were a stitch!

Getting to the marker gives you the opportunity to have a break, a cup of tea, or go to bed. Otherwise you may just keep knitting round, and round, and round...

The cast on is the top edge of the bag. To create a firm top edge, the first few rows are usually knitted on a smaller size circular needle than the main body of the bag. Often these first rows are worked in seed stitch to stop the edge curling. If the bag has a fluffy trim on the top edge, made with eyelash yarn, then the first few rows are purled to put more of the fibers on the right side.

I find knitting on circular needles almost hypnotic, as I get into a rhythm and feel that the knitted fabric is produced more quickly than if I work on straight needles.

You then change to a larger size needle for the main body of the bag, knitting every stitch on every round. However, rather than producing garter stitch—which is what would happen if you knitted every stitch on every row working with straight needles—when you knit every row on the circular needle, the fabric you make is stockinette stitch.

Many of the bags use a three-needle bind off; this binds off and joins the base at the same time. This bound off edge almost disappears when the bag is felted, creating a virtually invisible seam.

Anyone who suffers from arthritis may find knitting with circular needles easier than with straight needles, as the weight of the knitting is on the cord in your lap rather than on your wrists.

I find knitting on circular needles almost hypnotic, as I get into a rhythm and feel that the knitted fabric is produced more quickly than if I work on straight needles.

Circular needles are also more portable than longer straight needles, so you can happily knit on the bus or train without risk of poking your neighbor with the end of your knitting needle. If you have to stop for any reason, you can pull the ends of the needles up together and the work sits on the cord until you are ready to start again.

Knitting with double-pointed needles

Four or five double-pointed knitting needles are used to shape the base of some of the bags where there are not enough stitches to use a circular needle. The idea of knitting with more than two needles scares some people, but once you get the hang of it you will realize that you are still only using two needles at any given time; you can just ignore the ones that you aren't actually using.

Double-pointed needles come in sets of four or five, which makes it easy to divide the stitches between the needles. You should have the same, or a similar, number of stitches on each working needle. With four needles you divide the stitches between three of them and knit with the fourth. With five needles, you divide the stitches between four and knit with the fifth.

Usually, care has to be taken not to create a gap between the last stitch on one needle and the first stitch on the next, but for these bags this does not really matter so much, as the gaps will disappear once the piece is felted.

Two double-pointed needles are used for making the i-cord handles, as this is the quickest way to make the cords. I have used French knitting bobbins, but find using the double-pointed needles much quicker and more versatile as the number of stitches can be changed.

The felting process hides a multitude of sins—uneven gauge, twisted stitches, and even dropped stitches disappear.

felting the knitting

Once you have knitted your bag, you need to felt it. This isn't hard to do, as it's the washing machine that does the work for you. However, do read this section through and if you are using a substitute yarn (see page 113), knit and felt a swatch before making a bag.

The wool yarns that I use for the bags are pure merino wools that I import myself. They felt beautifully at 40 degrees to give a firm felt that holds its shape when dry. The yarns come in a wide range of colors and these colors can be knitted together to make yet more shades.

Because the wool yarns felt so well and so easily, other non-wool yarns can be knitted in with them and, providing the non-wool yarn is not thicker than the pure wool, it should felt well. The wool traps the non-wool yarn and still produces a firm enough felt to give the bag body. As the wool felts at 40 degrees, the acrylic yarns or non-wool yarns do not spoil, which they might do if they were felted at a higher temperature.

Being able to mix non-wool yarns with the pure wool allows you to add lots of texture and decoration. I have incorporated eyelash, feather, ribbon, sari silk, banana fiber, metallic, and sequinned yarns and they all have worked beautifully.

Before felting, the knitted bag will look very much like an ugly duckling, but it will turn out to be a swan! The bag will be much larger than you would expect, but it will shrink by approximately one-third in length and one-quarter in the width. The handles will look very long, almost ridiculously long, but they will shrink quite dramatically and firm up once felted.

I prefer to sew most of the embellishments on before felting—so that they actually felt into the bag and become an integral part of it—rather than sewing them on afterward. Use pure wool yarn and a knitter's sewing needle or bodkin

As this pre-felted version of an Anything Goes Stash Bag (see page 40) shows, before it is felted the knitting will be enormous and very floppy. But don't worry, it'll change completely once felted.

to sew on the embellishments. If I use buttons as a closure then I sew them on with wool yarn so that they felt into the bag and make a strong, secure fastening. Sew on snaps or other fasteners with wool yarn, too, and they will also felt into the bag. If the buttons are purely for decoration, I tend to sew them on after felting as they can move during the felting process.

Felting in the washing machine

This is where your floppy, huge, knitted thing turns into a gorgeous and practical felted bag.

I use a front-loading washing machine for felting my knitted bags. Choose a full 40 degree program, rather than a short program, as this gives the agitation needed to felt the bag. This agitation is very important, as it is this as well as the temperature that felts the wool. Some washing machines may need to be set at a higher temperature to get perfect results. The 40 degree program turns the Knitting4fun yarns into a firm felt, which I like, but if you prefer a lighter felt, then you can experiment with shorter washes and different temperatures.

I do use laundry detergent and usually put the bag in an empty washing machine—rather than in with other items such as towels, jeans, or old sneakers—as I think a bag felts better by itself. You can place the bag in an empty pillowcase to stop any fibers clogging up the filter, particularly when using mohair yarn. If you can open the filter easily it is best to clean it regularly so as not to clog it up and possibly cause damage to the washing machine.

Spin the bag dry then take it out of the washing machine as soon as possible. Do not allow the bag to sit in the machine for too long or creases may appear. If, after going through the wash program, the bag has not felted enough, try putting it through again at the same temperature rather than at a higher temperature. If that does not work, then try a higher temperature. Once it is fully felted, the bag will shrink by about one-third in length and one-quarter in width. You must consider this shrinkage when designing your own bag patterns.

The bag will now need to be stretched into shape: I use tins or cartons to do this. You must shape the bag while it is damp as once it is dry it cannot be shaped without dampening it again. Place the tins in the damp bag so that the felt is taut and the bag is the desired shape. Leave the tins in the bag while it dries, placing it on the windowsill or a radiator. If the handles have shrunk a little too much, hang the bag from a radiator with the tins still inside so that the weight of them stretches the handles while they dry.

If the handles do not felt firmly enough, try holding the damp bag and hitting the handles against the wall outside the house. This seems to shock the wool and firms it up. You can also do this to the body of the bag if it has not felted enough. Just be aware of the neighbors or the mailman, as they will think you are crazy, beating your handbag against the wall.

If the felted bag seems a little too fluffy, which it can do occasionally, depending on the yarns that have been used (mohair or alpaca are very hairy), I sometimes use hair clippers to shave the bag. I often do this outside so that the birds can have the fibers for their nests. This is when the neighbors and mailman do decide that I am completely crazy, because it's not every day you see a woman shaving her handbag on the doorstep!

I have not felted my bags by hand personally, but have had friends do this. You can wash the bag in warm water in a big saucepan and agitate it by stirring and by repeatedly throwing it into the sink to shock the wool. Rinse it under the cold tap and then the hot tap and keep throwing it into the sink or bashing it against the draining board, beating or "fulling" it until it is firmly felted.

abbreviations and conversions

A, B, C	colors as listed
alt	alternate; alternatively
approx	approximately
cont	continue
dc	double crochet
dec(s)	decrease(s)(ing)
foll(s)	follow(s)(ing)
in.	inch; inches
inc	increase(s)(ing)
k	knit
k2tog	knit two stitches (or number stated) together
M1	make one stitch by picking up horizontal strand between stitches with tip of left-hand needle, using right-hand needle, knit into back of picked up strand
MB	make bobble
oz	ounce(es)
p	purl
p2tog	purl two stitches (or number stated) together
patt(s)	pattern(s)
psso	pass the slipped stitch over the stitch just worked
rem	remain(ing)
rep	repeat
RS	right side
sc	single crochet
skpo	slip one stitch, knit one stitch, pass slipped stitch over
sk2po	slip one stitch, knit two stitches together, pass slipped stitch over
sl	slip
st st	stockinette stitch
st(s)	stitch(es)
tbl	through back of loop
tog	together

Needle sizes

There are three systems of sizing needles and here are the equivalent sizes across all three.

US	Metric	old UK and Canadian
50	25	–
35	19	–
19	15	–
15	10	000
13	9	00
11	8	0
11	7.5	1
10½	7	2
10½	6.5	3
10	6	4
9	5.5	5
8	5	6
7	4.5	7
6	4	8
5	3.75	9
4	3.5	–
3	3.25	10
2/3	3	11
2	2.75	12
1	2.25	13
0	2	14
00	1.75	–
000	1.5	–

resources

There is a huge range of yarns available to today's knitter by mail order over the Internet. Here is a list of suppliers of the yarns I have used in this book. You will find that many of these websites also have details of worldwide stockists.

Suppliers of yarns

Knitting4fun is my own yarn company. It was set up because I struggled to find the yarns I wanted to use. I tend to sell natural-fiber yarns and pure wools or wool blends. Many of the yarns are also fair trade yarns, particularly from South America and Nepal. Come and visit us at the website and see what we are up to.
www.knitting4fun.com

Webs
www.yarn.com

Halcyon Yarn
www.halcyonyarn.com

The complete range of Brown Sheep yarns.
www.brownsheep.com

The complete range of Cascade yarns.
www.cascadeyarns.com

The complete range of Colinettte yarns.
www.colinette.com

The complete range of Crystal Palace yarns, including Fjord Print Worsted Wool.
www.crystalpalaceyarns.com

The complete range of Noro yarns.
www.designeryarns.uk.com
Webs
www.yarn.com
Knitting Fever
www.knittingfever.com

The complete range of Elle yarns.
www.elleyarnsuk.com

The complete range of Filati yarns.
www.filatiyarn.com

The complete range of Ice yarns.
www.iceyarns.com

The complete range of Katia yarns.
www.katia.ee

The complete range of Lang yarns.
www.langyarns.ch/en

Karaoke Multi Wool Blend yarn.
www.soysilk.com

Suppliers of plastic bag handles
www.joggles.com
www.fabric.com
www.u-handbag.com

Suppliers of buttons
www.buttonsgaloreandmore.com

Suppliers of beads
www.artbeads.com
www.shipwreckbeads.com

These are two of my favorite yarn companies; they supply great ranges of lovely yarns.
www.creativeyarns.co.uk
www.yarnparadise.com

This is my favorite supplier of wonderful fabrics, notions, and wools, and they also stock Knitting4fun yarns.
www.heathscountrystore.co.uk

index

acknowledgments

This is my chance to say thank you to many of the people who have helped me along the way, but maybe they didn't realize they had.

My mother's godmother, Auntie Mo, and my grandmother, Ida, taught me knitting and crochet as a child, along with many other crafts, and my grandfather, Joe, used to buy me many of the materials I needed. I did not appreciate at the time how much he had encouraged me, too. Auntie Mo would take me into Nottingham and we would go into Bellman's yarn shop. There seemed to be a huge array of colors and little balls of wonderful yarns. I would be treated to some yarn and then to a drink and cake in a café. My yarn addiction started there, at such a young age.

I would like to thank my college tutors, Cherrilyn Tyler and Pauline Barke, who supported and encouraged me to explore my ideas and gave me the confidence to carry them out. Also Sandra Coleridge, whom I met through Valerie Campbell Harding when they were teaching together. They are all valued friends and mentors.

I would like to thank Jenny and Tanya for buying those first handbags from me when I certainly had no intention of selling my wares. My mum, Doreen, and sisters, Bernadette and Bridget, were great models for the bags and then became my sales team.

Thanks to Elaine and Julie, who gave me a job when I needed one, and for all their support and friendship.

My husband, Tom (Poor Tom, as he is now better known), and son, Frazer, who have had to suffer wool in almost every room in the house. Tom has been dragged (I think he enjoyed it really) to the knitting and yarn shows and has helped me tremendously, along with my mum and Karen and Gill.

I would like to thank all of the knitters I have met at our knitting groups, at shows, and over the Internet. Without you buying my patterns and kits I may not have ended up writing this book. We knitters come from all walks of life and knitting crosses generations: I have so many new friends, and hopefully many more to come, that I am grateful to knitting for that.

Thanks to Paula, Janet, Jane, and all of the team at Breslich & Foss for asking me to produce this book.

Special thanks to Kate Haxell, my editor, Sussie Bell, the photographer, and Elizabeth Healey, the designer, for making this book come alive.

I want to take this opportunity to thank Dr Claire Joynson and all of the oncology team at Leicester Royal Infirmary for their medical care, help, and support during my treatment for cancer. I was treated with respect, compassion, and importantly, as an individual. I truly felt that I had, and am still having, the best ever care. Many of the bags in this book were knitted during my stay at the hospital while undergoing the weeks of radiotherapy treatment.

As a foster carer I would also like to thank the children who have enriched our home over the past few years, some of you staying for only a few days and some of you for years. I will never forget you and have such fond memories. Many of you have also been introduced to the world of yarn and knitting by the mad wool woman with crazy colored hair.